LAW

THE BASICS

WITHDRAWN

Law: The Basics is an engaging introduction to one of the most complex areas of modern life. The book introduces both the main components of the legal system – including judges, juries, and law-makers – and key areas of law – contract, civil negligence, and criminal law – to provide the uninitiated with an ideal introduction to law. Key questions to be considered include:

- How are laws made?
- How do judges decide cases?
- What is the exact role of the EU in the legal system?
- What are your rights and duties under contract law?
- What is a crime and what are criminal defences?

Throughout the book, a wide range of contemporary cases are examined to relate key legal concepts to familiar examples and real world situations.

Gary Slapper is Professor of Law, and Director of the Law School, at The Open University. He is Visiting Professor of New York University, and at the Chinese University of Hong Kong. He is a door tenant at 36 Bedford Row and a legal columnist for *The Times*.

David Kelly was formerly Principal Lecturer in Law at the Staffordshire University Law School. They have written several books together including the Routledge textbooks *The English Legal System*, ' *Answers on the English Legal System*.

The Basics

ACTING
BELLA MERLIN

ANTHROPOLOGY
PETER METCALF

ARCHAEOLOGY (SECOND EDITION)
CLIVE GAMBLE

ART HISTORY
GRANT POOKE AND DIANA NEWALL

THE BIBLE
JOHN BARTON

BUDDHISM
CATHY CANTWELL

CRIMINAL LAW
JONATHAN HERRING

CRIMINOLOGY (SECOND EDITION)
SANDRA WALKLATE

ECONOMICS (SECOND EDITION)
TONY CLEAVER

EUROPEAN UNION (SECOND EDITION)
ALEX WARLEIGH-LACK

FILM STUDIES
AMY VILLAREJO

FINANCE (SECOND EDITION)
ERIK BANKS

HUMAN GENETICS
RICKI LEWIS

INTERNATIONAL RELATIONS
PETER SUTCH AND JUANITA ELIAS

ISLAM (SECOND EDITION)
COLIN TURNER

JUDAISM
JACOB NEUSNER

LANGUAGE (SECOND EDITION)
R. L. TRASK

LITERARY THEORY (SECOND EDITION)
HANS BERTENS

LOGIC
J. C. BEALL

MANAGEMENT
MORGEN WITZEL

MARKETING (SECOND EDITION)
KARL MOORE AND NIKETH PAREEK

PHILOSOPHY (FOURTH EDITION)
NIGEL WARBURTON

PHYSICAL GEOGRAPHY
JOSEPH HOLDEN

POETRY (SECOND EDITION)
JEFFREY WAINWRIGHT

POLITICS (FOURTH EDITION)
STEPHEN TANSEY AND NIGEL JACKSON

THE QUR'AN
MASSIMO CAMPANINI

RELIGION (SECOND EDITION)
MALORY NYE

RESEARCH METHODS
NICHOLAS WALLIMAN

ROMAN CATHOLICISM
MICHAEL WALSH

SEMIOTICS (SECOND EDITION)
DANIEL CHANDLER

SHAKESPEARE (SECOND EDITION)
SEAN MCEVOY

SOCIOLOGY
KEN PLUMMER

TELEVISION STUDIES
TOBY MILLER

TERRORISM
JAMES LUTZ AND BRENDA LUTZ

THEATRE STUDIES
ROBERT LEACH

WORLD HISTORY
PETER N. STEARNS

WORLD MUSIC
RICHARD NIDEL

LAW

THE BASICS

gary slapper and david kelly

Routledge
Taylor & Francis Group

LONDON AND NEW YORK

First published 2011
by Routledge
2 Park Square, Milton Park, Abingdon, Oxon OX14 4RN

Simultaneously published in the USA and Canada
by Routledge
711 Third Avenue, New York, NY 10017

Routledge is an imprint of the Taylor & Francis Group, an informa business

British Library Cataloguing in Publication Data
A catalogue record for this book is available from the British Library

Library of Congress Cataloging in Publication Data
Slapper, Gary.
  Law : the basics / Gary Slapper and David Kelly.
    p. cm. – (The Basics)
  Includes bibliographical references and index.
  1. Law – England. I. Kelly, David. II. Title.
  KD661.S585 2011
  349.42 – dc22
       2010053381

ISBN: 978-0-415-56805-0 (hbk)
ISBN: 978-0-415-56806-7 (pbk)
ISBN: 978-0-203-81041-5 (ebk)

Typeset in Bembo and Scala Sans
by Taylor & Francis Books

CONTENTS

LIST OF ABBREVIATIONS

ACSA	Anti-Terrorism, Crime and Security Act
ADR	alternative dispute resolution
ASBO	anti-social behaviour order
BME	black and minority ethnic
CJA	Criminal Justice Act
CPS	Crown Prosecution Service
DCA	Department for Constitutional Affairs
DPP	Director of Public Prosecutions
ECA	European Communities Act
ECHR	European Convention on Human Rights
ECJ	European Court of Justice
ECtHR	European Court of Human Rights
EEC	European Economic Community
HMCS	Her Majesty's Court Service
HRA	Human Rights Act
MOJ	Ministry of Justice
QC	Queen's Counsel
SEA	Single European Act
SoGA	Sale of Goods Act

ACKNOWLEDGMENTS

We owe a great gratitude to many people for the work and expertise that contributed to this book. We owe a particular debt to Suzanne, Hannah, Emily, Charlotte, Jane and Michael for their patience and support while we wrote.

We have benefited from the sustained encouragement and professionalism of Andrew Humphries, Senior Commissioning Editor at Routledge, who commissioned the book. The book benefitted from the work of Andrew Watts, our marvellous Production Editorial Manager, and from the work of Mary Dalton, our superb copy-editor.

We are indebted to Mel Dyer at RefineCatch for his vigilant professionalism. We also wish to thank Carolyn Bracknell, Abby Carr, Professor Dame Hazel Genn QC, Professor Michael Furmston, Lynn Tayton QC, and John Cooper QC, for their stimulating thoughts. In respect of human rights, we should particularly like to acknowledge the support of the Celtic connections: Miceál Barden, Angus McDonald, and Dewi Williams.

Lots of other people have offered encouragement, observations and assistance. Thanks are thus due to Doreen and Ivor Slapper, Clifford, Maxine, Pav, Anish, the late Raie Schwartz, David and Julie Whight, Professor Robert Reiner, Hugh McLaughlan, Ben Fitzpatrick, Robert Zimmerman, Jane Goodey, Carol Howells, Professor Jeffrey Jowell QC, Professor Ian Dennis, Professor Tony Lentin, Malcolm Park, Clare Hogan, Frances Gibb at *The Times*, and The Rt Hon The Lord Woolf.

PREFACE

The law is everywhere. A comic once observed that 'we used to have one law for the rich and one for the poor – but now we have hundreds of laws for everyone'. Although it is true that we have an abundance of laws, and thousands of legal procedures, it is possible to explain the basics of how the legal system works in a reasonable number of pages and that has been our aim here.

Organised legal education did not get off to a good start. It was condemned as unlawful and shut down just after it was launched in London. The monarch, Henry III, considered it would not be good to have people prying into the law and spreading opinions about its contents.

The law schools set up in London in the early thirteenth century were suppressed in 1234 by a writ of Henry. It said:

> Through the whole city of London let it be proclaimed and wholly forbidden that anyone who has a school of law in that town shall teach the laws ... and if anyone shall conduct a school of that nature there, the Mayor and the Sheriffs shall put a stop to it at once.

Today, by contrast, law is an enormously popular subject at universities and in colleges.

Roman law and church law were taught at the ancient universities for centuries but the systematic study of national law is a relatively new development, although the Inns of Court in London (collegiate institutions which all barristers must join) were frequently referred to in the seventeenth century as 'the legal university' and there was then no methodical teaching of English law at Oxford or Cambridge. Even by the early nineteenth century, legal education was nothing like it is today – being 'called to the Bar' to become a barrister was technically a process of simply eating and drinking at the Inn. Practically, the process involved learning the trade in the same way an apprentice would learn: by watching and helping. According to one contemporary description, the apprenticeship involved 'going into a pleaders' office for two or three years to learn to tell a plain story in very unintelligible language'.

Sir William Blackstone, arguably the first great English academic lawyer, had tried, as an Oxford professor in the eighteenth century, to establish English law as a distinct subject. In the event, it was the disciples of Jeremy Bentham who established the first degree in English law, at University College London (UCL) in 1826. The first graduating class of three was in 1839.

Now, law is the most applied for subject at university. The contents of law courses have always changed across time. Legal subjects develop largely in response to social developments. A society of computers and the internet, for example, gives us books on courses on computer law. In fact, however, large parts of the common subjects of today's law (like contract, tort, family law) have developed in quite recent history. As late as 1900, most of the legal academic subjects we have now either did not then exist or had very different syllabuses from courses with the same name today. As society changes, so the law has to adapt to such change, and, consequently so does legal scholarship, legal education and training. For example, criminal law is now a core part of law courses but specific syllabuses and books called 'criminal law' have been produced for only just over a century in the legal system's thousand-year history. Today areas of study and practice like sports law, media law, intellectual property law, immigration and asylum law, and international criminal justice are very important, whereas they did not exist as significant compartments of knowledge and jurisprudence, or courses, and were not the subject of legal literature, as recently as fifty years ago.

It is difficult to overstate the importance of law today. The law affects everyone in virtually every aspect of our lives. By understanding the law, it is possible to understand a great deal of how modern society works.

Gary Slapper
David Kelly
January 2011

TABLE OF CASES

TABLE OF STATUTES AND OTHER INSTRUMENTS

STATUES

STATUTORY INSTRUMENTS

EUROPEAN LEGISLATION

TREATIES AND CONVENTIONS

DIRECTIVES

TYPES OF LAW

There are many ways to divide law into different types. Putting law into categories is like putting people into categories – it can be done in different ways and for different purposes. If you take 100 random people in a crowd you could sort them into groups according to height, or weight, or age, or occupation, or skin colour, or blood type, or place of birth, or any number of other criteria. A 34-year-old, 5 ft 7 in., dark-haired female musician, weighing 8 stone, and born in Hong Kong with blood type O, would be placed among different subsets of people from the 100 depending on how people were being categorised.

In the same way, law can be put into different groups according to different criteria. The quantity of law that applies in the UK today is very considerable. It is contained in thousands of voluminous law reports of decided cases judged over many centuries, statutes and regulations passed by Parliament, and a gigantic quantity of European law and European human rights law.

Taking this law as a whole, it can be divided according to whether it has originated from judicial pronouncement (judge-made law) or legislation (from Parliament). Equally, it could be divided according to whether it is *private* law (law, like contract law, which applies to people in the private relations they might have as citizens or organisations) or *public* law (like criminal law which applies to everyone at large).

Very commonly, a single transaction or relationship or event will entail the relevance of a great many laws and several types of law. For example, consider the awful case of a lorry travelling at speed along a motorway, crashing into a car that had stopped on the hard shoulder, killing one of a number of people standing near the car, and then smashing through the barrier and plunging down an embankment on to a railway line in front of an oncoming train. All sorts of law could be applied to such a dreadful situation including the following:

- A criminal charge of dangerous driving against the lorry driver;
- A criminal charge of causing death through dangerous driving against the lorry driver;
- If defective brake pads and discs had been fitted to this lorry, along with others in the fleet owned by the haulage company, and it evidently knew of this danger, then there might be a charge of 'corporate manslaughter' against the haulage firm;
- A civil claim in the tort of negligence by the dependants of the person who was killed, against the lorry driver and his or her employer;
- A civil action in the tort of negligence for nervous shock by people who witnessed the horror of the carnage at its scene;
- A civil action for economic loss in the tort of negligence against the lorry driver and the haulage firm brought by the train company, or companies, whose business was disrupted for days following the terrible accident and the blocked train lines;
- The accident might well have prevented a number of scheduled events with a commercial significance from taking place. For example, if a pop group or orchestra was unable to arrive at a large auditorium to play on a scheduled night (as part of a busy world tour that would not be repeated) then various civil actions for breach of contract or insurance-related claims might follow, in which case the law relating to the frustration of contracts and so called 'Acts of God' might be applicable.

These last four claims would, if successful, be likely to be paid by the defendant's insurance companies.

What follows are a number of ways in which the law might be divided.

CRIMINAL LAW AND CIVIL LAW

Criminal cases are generally brought by the state for offences ranging from graffiti to murder. If the defendant is found guilty he or she is punished. Civil cases are brought by citizens or organisations and the aim is usually to get compensation or a court order to make someone do something or stop doing something.

CRIMINAL LAW

Ultimately, all justice systems hinge on their criminal codes because the criminal law is the portion of the law underpinning the legal system and enforcing its edicts. Behind every *civil law* court order is the force of a *criminal* sanction for disobedience of the order. Testimony in all civil, family, and private law matters is upheld ultimately by criminal laws against contempt of court, perjury, and perverting the course of public justice. There are many types of law but failing to obey a court which tries to enforce any of these types of law is ultimately a crime.

What is the distinguishing characteristic of a crime? What puts one type of wrong in the category of a crime, and keeps another as a civil wrong? The truth is that there is no scientific way of differentiating wrongs on that basis. It is impossible to be definitive about the nature of a crime because the essence of criminality changes with historical context. As one legal writer, Glanville Williams, observed (1983):

> a crime (or offence) is a legal wrong that can be followed by criminal proceedings which may result in punishment.

In ancient times, lending money and charging interest was the crime of usury. Now if done successfully it might earn a banker a knighthood. Cocaine used to be a legal narcotic used both for recreational purposes and toothache; now it is illegal.

If you ask 'what is a crime?' and are given the answer 'anything that can be punished as a crime', you might reply that such an answer keeps you going around in circles because you could then say 'yes, but what sort of things are likely to be labelled by the state as crimes and then punished?' In an attempt to escape from the circularity of these definitions of crime ('a crime is anything that is punished as a crime'), some writers have sought to explain its nature in terms of the seriousness of the conduct it prohibits.

Thus Glanville Williams eventually concedes (1983) that

a crime is an act that is condemned sufficiently strongly to have induced the authorities (legislature or judges) to declare it to be punishable before the ordinary courts.

This is a little more helpful but it still leaves unanswered the question – 'condemned sufficiently strongly' by whom? The principle connects with the thinking of the nineteenth-century French writer, Emile Durkheim. He remarked on the way that collective 'social consciousness' can be enhanced by the condemnation and punishment of deviance. People like to stick together to condemn what they see as wrong, and this behaviour strengthens their togetherness. Criminal law therefore bolsters social solidarity.

The *public* nature of crimes is evidenced by the fact that, technically, any citizen is permitted to bring a prosecution after a crime. He or she does not have to establish a *personal* interest as is necessary in civil proceedings. Each year there are about two million prosecutions, of which about 20 per cent are brought by someone other than the Crown Prosecution Service. These include shops, the education welfare service, utility companies and transport organisations. About 2 per cent of prosecutions are brought by private individuals.

By contrast to the general principle that anyone can prosecute for a crime, in civil law a litigant needs to show a particular status. For example, in *Holmes v Checkland* (1987) an opponent of cigarette smoking was denied 'standing' to restrain the BBC from broadcasting a snooker championship sponsored by a tobacco company, since he was no more affected than anyone else. He could only proceed with the aid of the Attorney-General. The word 'standing' in this context comes from the Latin phrase *locus standi*, 'a place to stand', which was used in older cases to denote that someone, by virtue of being personally affected by a matter, was in a position to sue.

There are only minimal controls over who can prosecute for a crime for the public good. There is provision in s. 24 of the Prosecution of Offences Act 1985 for the High Court, on the application of the

Attorney-General, to restrain a 'vexatious' prosecutor. A vexatious prosecutor means someone who by the serial nature of their prosecutions or the evident malice of them is denied the facility in future. Another control is that if a private prosecution is regarded as inappropriate by the governmental legal authorities, the Attorney-General can take it over, for the sole purpose of dropping it. That process is called *nolle prosequi* (Latin for 'not to wish to proceed').

However, if a citizen begins a prosecution, he or she may *not* discontinue it at will because, as was decided in *R v Wood* (1832), it is not only his concern but that of all citizens. If a prosecution succeeds and sentence is passed, a pardon cannot be granted by the instigator of the prosecution, it can only be granted by the Crown.

THE ORIGINS OF CRIMINAL LAW

There can be little doubt about the importance of the criminal law as a method of social control. As the Criminal Law Commissioners noted in 1843: 'The high and paramount importance of the Criminal Law consists in this consideration, that upon its due operation the enforcement of every other branch of the law ... depends.' This aspect of the criminal law's importance has not diminished over the last 150 years. It retains a crucial ideological significance as being *the* form of law in closest touch with the public, and something which reinforces their belief in the need for 'law'.

There are differing explanations accounting for the rise of criminal law as a distinct entity. Some writers have regarded the process as being a rather chaotic development. Harding, for example, looking at nineteenth-century changes, suggests (1966) that it was manufactured piecemeal by statutes 'listing offences with minute particularity which had long ago obscured any general principles'.

The church's influence over early medieval criminal law is illustrated by the fact that although sentences still retained the character of retribution or an equivalent, the retribution ceased to be directly linked to the loss of the victim based on his claim but acquired a higher general significance as a divine punishment. In this way the church attempted to associate the ideological motive of atonement with the material aspect of compensation for the injury, and thus to construct, from penal law based on the principle of private revenge, a more effective means of maintaining public discipline.

The notion of crime as a type of wrong associated with 'wickedness' or 'evil' was fostered by the early church and its doctrine of atonement by penance. It was under the Norman rule, after 1066, that the Crown started to take charge of the criminal courts to protect 'the King's peace'. The degree of royal control, however, was very limited because the initiative for bringing criminals to justice still lay with the victim and his or her kin.

Actions against the criminal, the 'appeal of felony', had retribution as their main object was that the felon's property was forfeited, his belongings to the King and his lands to his feudal Lord so there was no gain for the victim. The Crown guarded this right to prosecute jealously – it was an offence for a victim to settle privately (take cash from the culprit) without permission. It was the imperfections of the appeal procedure, and the resulting loss to the revenue when claimants started to disregard the felony and sue in the civil courts, that brought about the introduction, in the twelfth century, of a new straight criminal process at the option of the Crown. That was the start of the modern criminal justice system. Today, over a million cases are prosecuted every year, criminal law is a core part of every criminal law course at university, and the most famous branch of the law.

CIVIL LAW

Sometimes words carry different meanings according to the settings in which the word is used. For example the word 'rich' can mean quite different things depending upon what sentence it is within. The person possessing great financial or financially quantifiable wealth can be described as rich. A food or diet can be described as rich if it contains a large proportion of fat or eggs, or even spice. A voice is rich if it is mellow or deep. And where it is said of a person's assertion or statement 'that is rich coming from you' then rich means highly amusing or ludicrous. The phrase 'civil law' can mean different things depending on the context in which it is used.

Civil law can be used to connote Code law (as in France or America), and so to distinguish it from common law jurisdictions like the UK. In other circumstances, 'civil law' can be used to refer to Roman law. Most commonly though, in the UK, 'civil law' is used to refer to the sort of law used in civil proceedings. Common examples include cases for breach of contract, for nuisance, for negligence and for defamation. Such civil proceedings have the object of declaring or enforcing a right for the advantage of a person or company, or of recovering money or property.

This can be contrasted with an action in law which is a *criminal prosecution*, which we have examined earlier, and with a *public* or *administrative* law action. Criminal actions are brought on behalf of the state to condemn as criminal something affecting society at large. Similarly, public or administrative law actions are aimed at securing a benefit for the general public, for example to stop a nuisance which is disturbing the public at large.

In civil proceedings, the person or organisation bringing the action is known as the claimant (before the Civil Procedure Rules 1998 came into effect in 1999, a claimant was known as a plaintiff). If this litigation, often called a civil action, succeeds, the defendant will be found liable, and judgment for the claimant might require the defendant to pay compensation (damages) to the claimant or to comply with a court order to carry out the terms of a contract (an order of specific performance), or to do something or to refrain from doing something (an injunction).

Important areas of civil law include contract law and tort law.

THE LAW OF CONTRACT

A contract is a legally enforceable agreement. In very early human societies where people lived in small, family, kin or tribal communities, and everybody knew everyone else, it was unnecessary to have any framework of rules dealing with exactly at what point and in what circumstances an agreement was made, and how it should be enforced. The more complicated a society becomes, though, with many thousands of transactions each hour or every day between strangers, the more it needs to have a sophisticated law of contract. Each week in the United Kingdom, with a population of 60 million, there are hundreds of millions of contracts made. You make a contract every time you buy something in a shop, or on the internet, or every time you buy a train or bus ticket. One leading writer on contract has put it this way:

> Contracts come in different shapes and sizes. Some involve large sums of money, others trivial sums. Some are of long duration, while others are of short duration. The content of contracts varies enormously

and may include contracts of sale, hire purchase, employment and marriage.

(McKendrick 2003: 1)

If you read a book on the law of contract you will discover that there are many hundreds of possible points of contention concerning whether a contract has been properly made by two or more parties who have clearly consented to all of the same points in an agreement. Disputes can arise over whether the behaviour of one party is a breach, or tantamount to a breach, of the agreement, whether an agreement based on a mistake or misrepresentation should still enjoy the protection of the law of contract, and what remedies are available where a contract has been broken.

Here is an example of a case decided in the law of contract. Under general principles in the law of contract, if there is to be an enforceable agreement, then an acceptance of an offer must be communicated to the person who has made the offer. If I am to accept your offer I must communicate my acceptance to you. In *Entores v Miles Far East Corp* (1955), the court was concerned with the technicality of precisely *where* a deal for '100 tons of Japanese cathodes' had been completed because other matters swung on the question of in which city the deal had been made. The court had to consider at what point an acceptance made by telex (a precursor of the fax machine) in Amsterdam was 'communicated' to the person receiving the message in London. Was it communicated when it was typed in by the sender or when it was printed at the other end? The Court of Appeal decided the deal was made in London when the telex message was printed out in that office.

Lord Justice Denning said that if an oral acceptance is drowned out by an over-flying aircraft, so that the person making an offer cannot hear the acceptance, then there is no contract at that point. Where two people are negotiating on the phone and one makes an acceptance to the other but the line goes dead so the acceptance is not heard then, again, there is no contract because the acceptance has not been communicated. Where, however, the acceptance is made clearly and audibly but the person to whom it is said does not hear, a contract *is* concluded unless the person who has made the offer clearly says to the person making the acceptance that he did not hear what was said.

In the case of 'instantaneous communication' like telephone or here, telex, the acceptance was ruled to take place at the moment wh the acceptance is *received* by the person who has made the offer and at the place where the person who has made the offer is situated.

THE LAW OF TORT

The law of tort covers a wide range of civil wrongs which, broadly speaking, are the ways in which you can cause injury, damage or loss to someone or some organisation, apart from breaking a contract that you have with them. The unusual word 'tort' is an old French term meaning wrong. It comes from the Latin word *tortus* which means twisted or crooked. A person who commits a tort is known in law as a tortfeasor.

One of the largest areas of civil action within tort is the wrong of negligence. The caseload for the courts is heavy. Over 9,000 negligence actions were heard by the courts in 2005.

Civil actions for the tort of negligence include litigation arising from car accidents, sporting accidents and medical accidents. Actions in negligence are often brought against car drivers, health authorities, local education authorities, and sometimes against professionals such as accountants and lawyers. Other torts include defamation (libel and slander), private nuisance, assault, false imprisonment, trespass and 'passing off'. Passing off occurs where, through icons or logos or website styles, a business is conducted in such a way as to mislead the public into believing that its goods or services are those of another more famous business, as where a design or packaging trade mark is falsely used.

The liability of the owners and occupiers of land for injury caused to visitors on to their land or premises is another area of tort. Similarly, liability for damage caused by animals or defective products is within the compass of tort.

Negligence is a very developmental area of tort law. In 1932, in *Donoghue v Stevenson*, Lord Macmillan made a momentous declaration about the law of civil negligence. He said 'the grounds of action may be as various and manifold as human errancy; and the conception of legal responsibility may develop in adaptation to altering social conditions and standards'. And thus has the law developed.

The case of *Barber v Somerset County Council* (2004) illustrates the way in which the courts have applied old principles so as to develop the law. The House of Lords held that a local authority was in breach of its duty to its employee to take reasonable care to avoid injuring his health where it had become aware that his difficulties at work were having an adverse effect on his mental health, but had taken no steps to help him.

Mr Alan Barber had been employed by the local authority as a teacher. In September 1995, there was a restructuring of staffing at the school at which he was employed, and he was told that in order to maintain his salary level he would have to take on further responsibilities. He worked between 61 and 70 hours per week, and often had to work in the evenings and at weekends. In February 1996 he spoke of 'work overload' to the school's deputy head teacher, and in March and April consulted his GP about stress at work, and made enquiries about taking early retirement. In May, he was absent from work for three weeks, his absence certified by his GP as being due to stress and depression. On his return to work he met with the head teacher and the two deputy head teachers, and discussed the fact that he was not coping with his workload and felt that the situation was becoming detrimental to his health.

He was not met with an entirely sympathetic response and no steps were taken by the school to assist him. Between August and October, he again contacted his GP about stress on a number of occasions. In November 1996, after losing control and shaking a pupil, Mr Barber left the school and did not return. By then he was unable to work as a teacher, or to do any work other than undemanding part-time work.

The House of Lords decided in favour of Mr Barber and endorsed damages of £72,000. Mr Barber, an experienced and conscientious teacher, had been absent for three weeks with no physical ailment, such absence having been certified by his GP as being due to stress and depression. The duty of his employer to take some action had arisen in June or July 1996 when Mr Barber had seen members of the school's management team, and continued so long as nothing had been done to help him. The senior management team should have made enquiries about his problems and discovered what they could have done to ease them, and the fact that the school as a whole was facing severe problems, with all the teachers stressed and overworked, did not mean that there was nothing that could have been done to help Mr Barber.

COMMON LAW AND CIVIL LAW

These terms are used to distinguish two distinct legal systems and approaches to law. The use of the term common law in this context refers to all those legal systems that have adopted the historic English legal system.

One principal distinction to be made between common law and civil law systems is that the common law system is largely case-centred and heavily reliant on judges' interpretation of general principles, allowing scope for a policy-conscious and pragmatic approach to the particular problems that appear before the courts. The law can be developed on a case-by-case basis. On the other hand, the civil law system tends to be a codified body of general abstract principles which control the exercise of judicial discretion. In reality, both of these views are extremes, with the former over-emphasising the extent to which the common law judge can impose his discretion and the latter underestimating the extent to which continental judges have the power to exercise judicial discretion. The European Court of Justice, established, in theory, on civil law principles, is, in practice, increasingly recognising the benefits of establishing a body of case law. Although the European Court of Justice is not bound by the operation of the doctrine of precedent (where a case is decided in line with similar earlier cases), it still does not decide individual cases on an individual basis without reference to its previous decisions.

COMMON LAW AND EQUITY

This dichotomy (division into two) reflects the way in which law developed within the English legal system. Both common law and equity are types of law, in the sense that they are applied by judges in law courts. But they are different types of law, and so how they are applied, their 'grammar' of operation, and their vocabularies are distinct.

As the common law progressed, it became more formal and judges often became very insistent on exact procedures being followed even if injustice sometimes resulted. A modern analogy would be with a company or government department that refused to deal with your complaint because none of its existing forms was suitable even though you obviously had suffered a wrong. Also the common law courts were perceived to be slow, highly technical and very expensive. A trivial mistake in pleading a case could lose a good argument. How could people obtain justice, if not in the common law courts? The response was the development of equity.

Claimants (then called plaintiffs) unable to gain access to the common law courts appealed directly to the sovereign, and such pleas would be passed for consideration and decision to the Lord Chancellor who acted as 'the King's conscience'. As the common law courts became more formal and more inaccessible, pleas to the Chancellor correspondingly increased and eventually this resulted in the emergence of a specific court constituted to deliver 'equitable' or 'fair' decisions in cases which the common law courts declined to deal with. As had happened with the common law, the decisions of the courts of equity established principles which were used to decide later cases. So, it should not be thought that the use of equity meant that judges had discretion to decide cases on the basis of their personal idea of what was just in each case.

An almost obsessive attention to words is, however, sometimes something that principles of equity cannot correct. You are, in general, strictly bound by the words you agree to sign to in a contract. If you attack someone in writing publicly, the form of words you use might amount to libel. The law generally governs people with a precise application of words and legal forms. Hence, Portia's admonition in *The Merchant of Venice* (Act 4 Scene i):

> This bond here gives you no drop of blood; the words expressly are 'a pound of flesh'. If in cutting off the pound of flesh you shed one drop of Christian blood, your land and goods are by the law to be confiscated ...

From medieval times, only a limited range of claim forms or 'writs' was available, and litigants had to be very careful about choosing the correct form for their complaint, and filling it in properly. Litigation could be struck out if there was a spelling mistake on the form. Errors in Latin were fatal to a claim, as was the omission of a single punctuation mark. The moral justice of a case was often subordinate to its orthography. So, the omission of a single down-stroke or contraction sign or an error of Latin were fatal mistakes in a writ (the old form of legal action). One writ, for example, was invalidated because *inundare* – to overflow or flood – was misspelled as *inumdare*.

The pursuit of propriety with such apparent pettifogging still happens today. Consider the world of cars. In 2004, Vincent Ryan was given a fixed penalty notice by a car park attendant in Ipswich, Suffolk. He was ordered to pay a £30 penalty, even though he had purchased a ticket, because he had left the ticket upside down on his dashboard – the penalty notice had been marked 'not displaying a valid parking ticket'. The need for punctiliousness, though, sometimes favours the citizen. Thus, in 2003 the speeding conviction of the footballer Dwight Yorke was quashed by the High Court because he did not personally fill in the official form to confirm that he was the driver of the vehicle. A missing signature rendered the form inadmissible evidence.

Historically, there were a number of important conditions which a person seeking justice from the Court of Equity had to meet:

- He had to show that he could not receive justice in the common law courts.
- He had to show that he himself was without blame. This was called coming to the court with 'clean hands'. By contrast, claimants using the older common law courts did not have to show they were acting in a morally blamefree way.
- He had to show that he had not delayed in bringing his case before the court.

The division between the common law courts and the Court of Equity continued until they were eventually combined by the Judicature Acts 1873–75. Prior to this legislation, it was essential for a party to raise his action in the appropriate court, for example, the courts of law (as opposed to the Court of Equity) would not implement equitable principles. The Acts, however, provided that every court had the power and the duty to decide cases in line with common law and equity, with the latter being paramount in the final analysis.

The development of equity did not stop centuries ago. The innovation of major principles has occurred several times in recent history. One example is the case of *Central London Property Trust v High Trees Ltd* (1947). It holds that a person who is already in a contract, and who has made a promise by which he intentionally modifies his contractual rights against another party, will not be allowed to resile from such a promise. Normally, to be enforced, any promise needs to be given in exchange for something of value, but equity here does not make such a requirement.

Mr Justice Denning's doctrine of 'promissory estoppel' has affected hundreds of thousands of such situations since, either because people take legal advice before they try to go back on such a promise (made within an existing contract), or they just try to go back on their word and so get to learn about the principle through a lawyer once things have gone wrong.

COMMON LAW AND STATUTE LAW

As you have seen, the 'common law' is the law that has been created by the judges through the decisions in the cases they have heard. The judge and jurist Oliver Wendell Holmes Jr very aptly summed up the way such development works. He noted in *The Common Law* (1881):

> The life of the law has not been logic: it has been experience. The felt necessities of the time, the prevalent moral and political theories, intuitions of public policy, avowed or unconscious, even the prejudices which judges share with their fellow-men, have had a good deal more to do than the syllogism in determining the rules by which men should be governed.
>
> (Wendell Holmes 1991 [1881]: 1)

Statute law, on the other hand, refers to law that has been created by Parliament in the form of legislation. Although there has been a significant increase in statute law in the twentieth and twenty-first centuries, the courts still have an important role to play in creating and operating law generally and in determining the operation of legislation in particular.

PUBLIC LAW AND PRIVATE LAW

This dichotomy concerns the difference between law that applies to public institutions, or everyone at large, in contrast to law that applies to citizens in their relations with each other. Public law includes the law governing the government, the constitution of the UK, the administration of public authorities, and criminal law.

Private law includes the law of contract and the law affecting neighbours. This division, therefore, runs across others mentioned in this chapter. Below, the law of contract is examined as part of civil law, whereas here it can also be mentioned to exemplify private law. It is under this heading that something more should be said in detail about constitutional and administrative law.

CONSTITUTIONAL AND ADMINISTRATIVE LAW

Constitutional law concerns the relationship between the individual and the state, examined from a legal viewpoint. The United Kingdom does not have one written document which is 'the Constitution'. What amounts to the Constitution in the UK is a diverse collection of guidelines and rules. It was described in 1733 by Henry Bolingbroke (1678–1751), a Tory statesman, as:

> That assemblage of laws, institutions and customs, derived from certain fixed principles of reason, directed to certain fixed objects of public good, that compose the general system, according to which the community have agreed to be governed.

Much of administrative law is concerned with the process of judicial review. Judicial review is the procedure by which prerogative (coming from the inherent power of the court, and not subject to restriction) and other remedies have been obtainable in the High Court against inferior courts, tribunals and administrative authorities. Its primary purpose is to control any actions of these bodies that might be made in excess of their proper powers or on the basis of some unreasonable way of coming to a decision.

In cases of judicial review an applicant will be proceeding against a public authority or part of the government asking for an official decision to be reviewed by a judge in respect of the propriety with which the decision was taken. In these cases judges can issue court orders of a mandatory, prohibiting or quashing variety (in earlier cases before 2000 these were known as orders of *mandamus* prohibition and *certiorari* respectively). In matrimonial cases the parties are called petitioner (who brings the action) and respondent (who defends it). The relief sought in the actions concerns dissolution of marriage.

Judicial review has expanded dramatically as a part of law in recent history. In 1981, 552 applications for judicial review were made at the High Court, whereas in 2004, a total of 4,207 applications were made.

The case of *John Hirst v United Kingdom* (2005) decided by the European Court of Human Rights (ECtHR) provides a good illustration of public law in action. In this important judgment the Strasbourg judges ruled by twelve to five that the denial of the right to vote to 48,000 sentenced prisoners in Britain amounted to an abuse of the right to free elections. The ruling challenged the 1870 Forfeiture Act, which introduced the Victorian punishment of 'civic death'. The idea was that upon imprisonment an inmate ceased to have any civil status. The court merely 'challenged' the law of 1870 because it cannot cancel British legislation.

Mr Hirst brought the case to ensure that MPs took an interest in what happened in their local prisons. The ECtHR ruled that voting was a protected human right and not a privilege, and awarded Mr Hirst £8,000 in costs and expenses. The court did not state that *all* prisoners must now be given the right to vote. The judges ruled that the UK government was wrong not to have considered fully the legal basis of its ban on prisoners voting, and whether it applied regardless of the gravity of the offence for which a prisoner had been convicted.

Many prisons are in marginal seats (political constituencies in which no political party has a clear primacy in popularity) and 600 or 700 votes from prisoners could swing the result. The ECtHR ruling will require legal changes by the UK government before it has any effect. It will eventually mean that prisoners' rights and interests will become more politically important as those fighting for seats in the House of Commons seek to gain prisoners' votes. Any candidate, however, seen to be according too much attention to such votes might be opposed by a rival who, by denying any promises to the prisoners, sought to win extra votes from other parts of the con-stituency. Whatever the outcome of such debates, the discussion will be lively.

There are, as we have seen, many types of law. In the next chapter we turn to look at how a particular mode of law – legislation – is made by Parliament.

2

HOW LAWS ARE MADE

INTRODUCTION

There are two main sources of law: legislation and case law. Our legal system is said to be a common law system and shares many characteristics with other jurisdictions such as the United States, and many other Commonwealth and former Commonwealth countries. Common law refers to the substantive law and procedural rules that have been created by the judiciary through the decisions in the cases they have heard. The common law tends to be case-centred and hence judge-centred, allowing scope for a discretionary, pragmatic approach to the particular problems that come before the courts (see chapter 4 below).

Statute law, on the other hand, refers to law that has been created by Parliament in the form of legislation. Although there has been a significant increase in statute law in the twentieth and twenty-first centuries, the courts still have an important role to play in creating and operating law generally and in determining the operation of legislation in particular. This distinction has a practical effect on where one looks to find the law. In common law systems one has to look in the reports of the cases decided in the courts as well as in the legislation made by Parliament. Nonetheless it has to be recognised that even though we still refer to our system as a common law one, due to the doctrine of parliamentary sovereignty statute law or legislation is superior to the law made by the judges in cases and is the predominant method of law-making in contemporary times. For that reason legislation will be considered before case law.

LEGISLATION

Under UK constitutional law, it is recognised that Parliament has the power to enact, revoke or alter such, and any, law as it sees fit. This is known as the doctrine of parliamentary sovereignty and it is one of the cornerstones of the UK constitution. In effect it means that, as long as the appropriate procedures are followed, Parliament is free to make such law as it determines. One corollary of the doctrine is that no current parliament can bind the discretion of a later parliament to make/change law as it wishes. Even the Human Rights Act (HRA) 1998, which will also be considered in some detail below, reaffirms this fact in its recognition of the power of Parliament to make primary legislation that is incompatible with the rights provided under the European Convention on Human Rights (ECHR). As will also be considered later, there is some debate about the powers of Parliament to make such law as it wishes within the context of the UK's membership of the European Union.

PARTS OF AN ACT

When a piece of legislation is in its draft stages, before it has been passed by Parliament, it is called a Bill and each part is called a 'clause' (sometimes abbreviated to 'Cl.'). Once the Bill has been passed, it is called an Act and each part is called a 'section' abbreviated to 's.'. Sometimes a section is subdivided into subsections and a subsection can itself be subdivided in paragraphs. Consider this example. Here is part of s. 1 of the Bribery Act 2010:

1   Offences of bribing another person
   (1)   A person ('P') is guilty of an offence if either of the following cases applies.
   (2)   Case 1 is where—
      (a)   P offers, promises or gives a financial or other advantage to another person, and

    (b) P intends the advantage—

        (i) to induce a person to perform improperly a relevant function or activity, or

        (ii) to reward a person for the improper performance of such a function or activity.

The extracted part would be referred to by lawyers as 'section 1, subsection 2, paragraph (a) of the Act'.

TYPES OF LEGISLATION

Legislation can be categorised in a number of ways. For example, distinctions can be drawn between the following:

- *Public Acts*, which relate to matters affecting the general public. These can be further subdivided into either government Bills or Private Members' Bills.
- *Private Acts*, on the other hand, relate to the powers and interests of particular individuals or institutions, although the provision of statutory powers to particular institutions can have a major effect on the general public. For example, companies may be given the power to appropriate private property through compulsory purchase orders.
- *Enabling legislation* gives power to a particular person or body to oversee the production of the specific details required for the implementation of the general purposes stated in the parent Act. These specifics are achieved through the enactment of secondary or *delegated legislation* (see below for a consideration of delegated legislation).

Acts of Parliament can also be distinguished on the basis of the function they are designed to carry out. Some are *unprecedented* and cover new areas of activity previously not governed by legal rules, but other Acts are aimed at *rationalising* or *amending* existing legislative provisions.

- *Consolidating legislation* is designed to bring together provisions previously contained in a number of different Acts, without actually altering them. The Companies Act of 1985 was an example of a consolidating Act. It brought together provisions contained in numerous amending Acts that had been introduced since the previous Consolidation Act of 1948. As well, the new Companies Act 2006 consolidated some previous legislation passed since the 1985 Act, but as it also contains previous common law provisions it may be seen as an example of the next category.

- *Codifying legislation* seeks not just to bring existing statutory provisions under one Act, but to give statutory expression to common law rules. Classic examples of such legislation are the Partnership Act of 1890 and the Sale of Goods Act 1893 (now 1979).

- *Amending legislation* is designed to alter some existing legal provision. Amendment of an existing legislative provision can take two forms:

    (i) a *textual amendment* is one where the new provision substitutes new words for existing ones in a legislative text or introduces completely new words into that text. Altering legislation by means of textual amendment has one major drawback, in that the new provisions make very little sense on their own, without the contextual reference of the original provision they are designed to alter;

    (ii) *non-textual amendments* do not alter the actual wording of the existing text, but alter the operation or effect of those words. Non-textual amendments may have more immediate meaning than textual alterations, but they too suffer from the problem that, because they do not alter the original provisions, the two provisions have to be read together to establish the legislative intention.

Neither method of amendment is completely satisfactory, but the Renton Committee on the Preparation of Legislation favoured textual amendments over non-textual amendments.

THE DRAFTING OF LEGISLATION

In 1975, in response to criticisms of the language and style of legislation, the Renton Committee on the Preparation of Legislation (Cmnd 6053) examined the form in which legislation was presented. Representations were made to the Committee by a variety of people ranging from the judiciary to the lay public. The Committee divided complaints about statutes into four main headings relating to:

- obscurity of language used;
- over-elaboration of provisions;
- illogicality of structure;
- confusion arising from the amendment of existing provisions.

It was suggested that the drafters of legislation tended to adopt a stylised archaic legalism in their language and employed a grammatical structure that was too complex and convoluted to be clear, certainly to the layperson and even, on occasion, to legal experts. These criticisms, however, have to be considered in the context of the whole process of drafting legislation and weighed against the various other purposes to be achieved by statutes. The actual drafting of legislation is the work of parliamentary counsel to the Treasury, who specialise in this task.

THE LEGISLATIVE PROCESS

THE PRE-PARLIAMENTARY PROCESS

Any consideration of the legislative process must be placed in the context of the political nature of Parliament. Most statutes are the outcome of the policy decisions taken by government, and the actual policies pursued will of course depend upon the political persuasion and imperatives of the government of the day. Thus, a great deal of law creation and reform can be seen as the implementation of party-political policies.

As, by convention, the government is drawn from the party controlling a majority in the House of Commons, it can effectively decide what policies it wishes to implement and trust to its majority to ensure that its proposals become law. Accusations have been made that when governments have substantial majorities, they are able to operate without taking into account the consideration of their own party members, let alone the views of Opposition members. It is claimed that their control over the day-to-day procedure of the House of Commons, backed by their majority voting power, effectively reduces the role of Parliament to that of merely rubber-stamping their proposals.

The government generates most of the legislation that finds its way onto the statute book, but individual Members of Parliament may also propose legislation in the form of Private Members' Bills. There are in fact three ways in which an individual Member of Parliament can propose legislation:

- through the ballot procedure, by means of which 20 backbench Members get the right to propose legislation on the 10 or so Fridays in each parliamentary session specifically set aside to consider such proposals;
- under Standing Order 39, which permits any Member to present a Bill after the 20 balloted Bills have been presented;
- under Standing Rule 13, the 10-minute rule procedure, which allows a Member to make a speech of up to 10 minutes in length in favour of introducing a particular piece of legislation.

Of these procedures, however, only the first has any real chance of success and even then success will depend on securing a high place in the ballot and on the actual proposal not being too contentious. Examples of this include the Abortion Act 1967, which was introduced as a Private Member's Bill to liberalise the provision of abortion, and the various attempts that have subsequently been made by Private Members' Bills to restrict the original provision.

The decision as to which government Bills are to be placed before Parliament in any session is under the effective control of two Cabinet committees:

- the *Future Legislation Committee* determines which Bills will be presented to Parliament in the *following* parliamentary session;
- the *Legislation Committee* is responsible for the legislative programme conducted in the *immediate* parliamentary session. It is the responsibility of this Committee to draw up the legislative programme announced in the Queen's Speech, delivered at the opening of the parliamentary session.

Green Papers are consultation documents issued by the government, which set out and invite comments from interested parties on particular proposals for legislation. After considering any response, the government may publish a second document in the form of a White Paper, in which it sets out its firm proposals for legislation.

PARLIAMENTARY PROCESS

Parliament consists of three distinct elements: the House of Commons, the House of Lords and the monarch. Before any legislative proposal, known at that stage as a Bill, can become an Act of Parliament, it must proceed through and be approved by both Houses of Parliament and must receive the Royal Assent. The ultimate location of power, however, is the House of Commons, which has the authority of being a democratically elected institution.

A Bill must be given three readings in both the House of Commons and the House of Lords before it can be presented for the Royal Assent. It is possible to start the procedure in either House, although money Bills must be placed before the Commons in the first instance.

When a Bill is introduced in the Commons, it undergoes five distinct procedures:

- *First reading*. This is purely a formal procedure in which its title is read and a date set for its second reading.
- *Second reading*. At this stage, the general principles of the Bill are subject to extensive debate. The second reading is the critical point in the process of a Bill. At the end, a vote may be taken on its merits and, if it is approved, it is likely that it will eventually find a place on the statute book.
- *Committee stage*. After its second reading, the Bill is passed to a standing committee whose job it is to consider its provisions in detail, clause by clause. The committee has the power to amend it in such a way as to ensure that it conforms with the general approval given by the House at its second reading. Very occasionally, a Bill may be passed to a special standing committee which considers the issues involved before going through the Bill in the usual way as a normal standing committee. Also, the whole House may consider certain Bills at committee stage. In general, these are Bills of constitutional importance, such as the House of Lords Bill, which proposed the reformation of the upper House

in 1999. Other Bills that need to be passed very quickly and certain financial measures, including at least part of each year's Finance Bill, are also considered by the committee of the whole House.

- *Report stage.* At this point, the standing committee reports the Bill back to the House for consideration of any amendments made during the committee stage.
- *Third reading.* Further debate may take place during this stage, but it is restricted to matters relating to the content of the Bill; questions relating to the general principles of the Bill cannot be raised.

When a Bill has completed all these stages, it is passed to the House of Lords for its consideration. After consideration by the Lords, the Bill is passed back to the Commons, which must then consider any amendments to the Bill that might have been introduced by the Lords. Where one House refuses to agree to the amendments made by the other, Bills can be repeatedly passed between them but, as Bills must usually complete their process within the life of a particular parliamentary session, a failure to reach agreement within that period might lead to the total loss of the Bill.

THE PARLIAMENT ACTS

Given the need for legislation to be approved in both Houses of Parliament, it can be seen that the House of Lords has considerable power in the passage of legislation. However, the fact that it was never a democratically accountable institution, together with the fact that until 2005 it had an in-built Conservative party majority reflecting its previous hereditary composition, meant that its legislative powers had to be curtailed. Until the early years of the twentieth century, the House of Lords retained its full power to prevent the passage of legislation. However, Lloyd-George's Liberal budget of 1909 brought the old system to breaking point when the House of Lords originally refused to pass it. Although the budget was eventually passed after a general election in 1910, a second election was held on the issue of reform of the House of Lords. As a result of the Liberal victory the Parliament Act of 1911 was introduced, which removed the House of Lords' power to veto a Bill. The Parliament Act of 1911 reduced the power of the Lords to the ability to delay a bill by up to two years. In 1949 the Parliament Act of that year further reduced the Lords' delaying powers to one year.

Since 1949 the delaying powers of the House of Lords have been as follows:

- a 'Money Bill', that is, one containing only financial provisions, can be enacted without the approval of the House of Lords after a delay of one month;
- any other Bill can be delayed by one year.

Only four substantive acts have been passed into law without the consent of the House of Lords:

- The War Crimes Act 1991
- The European Parliamentary Elections Act 1999
- The Sexual Offences (Amendment) Act 2000
- The Hunting Act 2004

REFORM OF THE HOUSE OF LORDS

The 1997 Labour government was elected on the promise of the fundamental reform of the House of Lords, which it saw as undemocratic and unrepresentative. After establishing a Royal Commission, the government embarked on a two-stage process of reform. The first stage of reform was achieved through the House of Lords Act 1999, which removed the right of the majority of hereditary peers to sit in the House of Lords. The second part of the reform was never completed as there was disagreement as to the extent to which the membership of the House of Lords should be elected or appointed. The recently elected coalition government's policy on reform of the House of Lords faced the problem of combining the two parties' manifesto proposals; the Conservatives preferring a 'mainly-elected second chamber', and the Liberal Democrats a 'fully-elected second chamber'.

In the spirit of (necessary) compromise the Prime Minister announced the establishment of a cross-party committee which would 'recommend the proportion of elected members in the new house who would be elected by proportional representation'.

ROYAL ASSENT

The Royal Assent is required before any Bill can become law. There is no constitutional rule requiring the monarch to assent to any Act passed by Parliament. There is, however, a convention to that effect, and refusal to grant the Royal Assent to legislation passed by Parliament would place the constitutional position of the monarchy in jeopardy. The procedural nature of the Royal Assent was highlighted by the Royal Assent Act 1967, which reduced the process of acquiring Royal Assent to a formal reading out of the short title of any Act in both Houses of Parliament.

COMMENCEMENT

An Act of Parliament comes into effect on the date of the Royal Assent, unless there is any provision to the contrary in the Act itself. It is quite common either for the Act to contain a commencement date for some time in the future, or for it to give the appropriate secretary of state the power to give effect to its provisions at some future time by issuing statutory instruments. The secretary of state is not required to bring the provisions into effect and it is not uncommon for some parts of Acts to be repealed before they are ever in force.

A current example of this failure to implement legislative provisions may be seen in the Equality Act 2010, one of the last pieces of legislation passed by the previous government. Although the new coalition Home Secretary, and Minister for Women and Equality, brought most of the provisions into effect through commencement orders, she let it be known that she would not do so with all its provisions and certainly not section 1 of the Act, which imposed a duty on public bodies to have due regard when making strategic decisions to reducing the inequalities of outcome which result from socio-economic disadvantage. In response critics accused her of rendering the Act 'virtually toothless'.

DELEGATED OR SUBORDINATE LEGISLATION

Generally speaking, delegated legislation is law made by some person or body to whom Parliament has delegated its general law-making power. A validly enacted piece of delegated legislation has the same legal force and effect as the Act of Parliament under which it is enacted but, equally, it only has effect to the extent that its enabling Act authorises it.

The output of delegated legislation in any year greatly exceeds the output of Acts of Parliament. For example, in the parliamentary year 2008, only 33 general public Acts were passed, as against well over 3,000 statutory instruments. When the contribution of the Scottish Parliament and the Welsh Assembly is included the number of pieces of secondary legislation is increased by almost a further 500, so there are usually 100 times as many pieces of secondary legislation as there are pieces of primary legislation.

TYPES OF DELEGATED LEGISLATION

There are various types of delegated legislation:

- *Orders in Council* permit the government through the Privy Council to make law. The monarch is present at many of these monthly meetings but can use deputies from among the heirs to the throne. The Privy Council is nominally a non-party-political body of eminent parliamentarians, but in effect it is simply a means through which the government, in the form of a committee of ministers, can introduce legislation without the need to go through the full parliamentary process. Although it is usual to cite situations of state emergency as exemplifying occasions when the government will resort to the use of Orders in Council, in fact, a great number of Acts are brought into operation through these Orders. Perhaps the widest scope for Orders in Council is to be found in relation to EU law, for under s. 2(2) of the European Communities Act 1972, ministers can give effect to provisions of the EU which do not have direct effect.
- *Statutory instruments* are the means through which government ministers introduce particular regulations under powers delegated to them by Parliament in enabling legislation.
- *Bylaws* are the means through which local authorities and other public bodies can make legally binding rules. Bylaws may be made by local authorities under such enabling legislation as the Local Government Act 1972.

- *Court Rule Committees* are empowered to make the rules which govern procedure in the particular courts over which they have delegated authority, under such Acts as the Senior Court Act 1981, the County Courts Act 1984 and the Magistrates' Courts Act 1980.
- *Professional regulations* governing particular occupations may be given the force of law under provisions delegating legislative authority to certain professional bodies who are empowered to regulate the conduct of their members. An example is the power given to The Law Society, under the Solicitors' Act 1974, to control the conduct of practising solicitors.

ADVANTAGES IN THE USE OF DELEGATED LEGISLATION

The advantages of delegated legislation include the following:

TIME SAVING

Delegated legislation can be introduced quickly, where necessary, in particular cases, and can permit rules to be changed in response to emergencies or unforeseen problems. The use of delegated legislation, however, also saves parliamentary time generally. Given the pressure on debating time in Parliament and the highly detailed nature of typical delegated legislation, not to mention its sheer volume, Parliament would not have time to consider each individual piece of law that is enacted in the form of delegated legislation. It is considered of more benefit for Parliament to spend its time in a thorough consideration of the principles of the enabling Act, leaving the appropriate minister or body to establish the working detail under its authority.

ACCESS TO PARTICULAR EXPERTISE

Related to the first advantage is the fact that the majority of Members of Parliament simply do not have sufficient expertise to consider such provisions effectively. Given the highly specialised and extremely technical nature of many of the regulations that are introduced through delegated legislation, it is necessary that those authorised to introduce the legislation should have access to the necessary external expertise required to formulate such regulations. With regard to bylaws, it practically goes without saying that local and specialist knowledge should give rise to more appropriate rules than reliance on the general enactments of Parliament.

FLEXIBILITY

The use of delegated legislation permits ministers to respond on an *ad hoc* basis to particular problems, as and when they arise, and provides greater flexibility in the regulation of activity subject to the minister's overview.

DISADVANTAGES IN THE PREVALENCE OF DELEGATED LEGISLATION

The disadvantages in the use of delegated legislation include the following:

ACCOUNTABILITY

A key issue involved in the use of delegated legislation concerns the question of accountability and erosion of the constitutional role of Parliament. Parliament is presumed to be the source of legislation, but with respect to delegated legislation, the individual members are not the source of the law. Certain people, notably government ministers and the civil servants who work under them to produce the detailed provisions of delegated legislation, are the real source of such regulations. Even allowing for the fact that they are, in effect, operating on powers delegated to them from Parliament, it is not beyond questioning whether this procedure does not give them more power than might be thought appropriate, or indeed con- stitutionally correct, while at the same time disempowering and discrediting Parliament as a body.

SCRUTINY

The question of general accountability raises the need for effective scrutiny, but the very form of delegated legislation makes it extremely difficult for ordinary Members of Parliament to fully understand what is being enacted and to monitor it effectively. This difficulty arises in part from the tendency for such regulations to be highly specific, detailed and technical. This problem of comprehension and control is compounded by the fact that regulations appear outside the context of their enabling legislation, but only have any real meaning within that context.

The problem faced by ordinary Members of Parliament in effectively keeping abreast of delegated legislation is further increased by its sheer mass. If parliamentarians cannot keep up with the flow of delegated legislation, how can the general public be expected to do so?

CONTROL OF DELEGATED LEGISLATION

The foregoing difficulties and potential shortcomings in the use of delegated legislation are, at least to a degree, mitigated by the fact that specific controls have been established to oversee it:

PARLIAMENTARY CONTROL OVER DELEGATED LEGISLATION

Power to make delegated legislation is ultimately dependent upon the authority of Parliament and Parliament retains general control over the procedure for enacting such law. New regulations in the form of delegated legislation are required to be laid before Parliament. This procedure takes two forms depending on the provision of the enabling legislation. Some regulations require a positive resolution of one or both of the Houses of Parliament before they become law. Most Acts, however, simply require that regulations made under their auspices be placed before Parliament. They automatically become law after a period of 40 days unless a resolution to annul them is passed.

The problem with the negative resolution procedure is that it relies on Members of Parliament being sufficiently aware of the content, meaning and effect of the detailed provisions laid before them. Given the nature of such statutory legislation, such reliance is unlikely to prove secure.

Since 1973, there has been a *Joint Select Committee on Statutory Instruments* whose function it is to scrutinise all statutory instruments. The Joint Committee is empowered to draw the special attention of both Houses to an instrument on any one of a number of grounds specified in the Standing Orders (No. 151 of the House of Commons and No. 74 of the House of Lords) under which it operates, or on any other ground *which does not relate to the actual merits of the instrument or the policy it is pursuing*.

The House of Commons has its own *Select Committee on Statutory Instruments*, which is appointed to consider all statutory instruments laid *only* before the House of Commons. This committee is empowered to draw the special attention of the House to an instrument on any one of a number of grounds specified in Standing Order No. 151; or on any other ground. However, as with the joint committee, it is not empowered to consider the merits of any statutory instrument or the policy behind it. As an example of its operation, after considering two statutory instruments, namely *Personal Equity Plan (Amendment No. 2) Regulations 2005 (SI 2005/3348)* and *Individual Savings Account (Amendment No. 3) Regulations 2005 (SI 2005/3350)*, the Committee considered that they should be drawn to the attention of the House of Commons on the ground that there appeared to be a doubt whether they were *intra vires*.

EU legislation is overseen by a specific committee as are local authority bylaws. In 2003 the House of Lords established a *Committee on the Merits of Statutory Instruments*, the task of which is to consider the policy implications of Statutory Instruments. It has wide-ranging remit and is specifically charged with the task of deciding whether the attention of the House should be drawn to a particular statutory instrument on any one of the following grounds:

- that it is politically or legally important or gives rise to issues of public policy likely to be of interest to the House;
- that it is inappropriate in view of the changed circumstances since the passage of the parent Act;
- that it inappropriately implements EU legislation;
- that it imperfectly achieves its policy objectives.

JUDICIAL CONTROL OF DELEGATED LEGISLATION

It is possible for delegated legislation to be challenged through the procedure of judicial review, on the basis that the person or body to whom Parliament has delegated its authority has acted in a way that exceeds the limited powers delegated to them. Any provision outside this authority is *ultra vires* and is void. Additionally, there is a presumption that any power delegated by Parliament is to be used in a reasonable manner, and the courts may on occasion hold particular delegated legislation to be void on the basis that it is unreasonable. However, an interesting example of this procedure may illustrate the point. In January 1997, the Lord Chancellor raised court fees and, at the same time, restricted the circumstances in which a litigant could be exempted from paying such fees. In March, a Mr John Witham, who previously would have been exempted from paying court fees, successfully challenged the Lord Chancellor's action. In a judicial review, it was held that Lord Mackay had exceeded the statutory powers given to him by Parliament. One of the judges, Rose LJ, stated that there was nothing to suggest that Parliament ever intended 'a power for the Lord Chancellor to prescribe fees so as to preclude the poor from access to the courts'.

The power of the courts in relation to delegated legislation has been considerably increased by the enactment of the Human Rights Act (HRA) 1998 (see below, chapter 3). As will be seen, the courts cannot directly declare primary legislation invalid, but can only issue a declaration of incompatibility. However, no such limitation applies in regard to subordinate legislation, which consequently may be declared invalid as being in conflict with the rights provided under the ECHR. This provision significantly extends the power of the courts in relation to the control of subordinate legislation, in that they are no longer merely restricted to questioning such legislation on the grounds of procedure, but can now assess it on the basis of content, as measured against the rights provided in the ECHR. It should be noted that Orders in Council as expressions of the exercise of the royal prerogative are not open to challenge and control in the same way as other subordinate legislation.

Having looked at how legislation is made we now move to look, in the next chapter, at how judges and lawyers interpret these laws.

3

MAKING SENSE OF LEGISLATION

The law written on the pages of legislation does not always have a real, concrete meaning until there is a dispute about whether it covers some real life event, and a law court declares the answer.

Acts of Parliament are of enormous importance. There are many thousands of them; Parliament is producing more than two thousand pages of new statutory law a year, and there is no limit on what law they can make.

In the UK, there is no law, like a Constitution, of higher authority or more deeply entrenched than an ordinary Act of Parliament. So there is no criterion by which an Act of Parliament can be judged as invalid, provided it has been properly passed using the correct procedure. Even an Act of Parliament passed to limit the life of governments to five years – like the Parliament Act 1911 – is only an ordinary Act of Parliament, with exactly the same status as the Wild Mammals (Protection) Act 1996.

So, any Act can be repealed and replaced with another Act proclaiming something different. An Act which began 'This Act is irrevocable and will have permanent standing in the UK' would be just as easy to repeal as any other Act.

In one case Lord Justice Kay said (*Metropolitan Railway Co v Fowler*, 1892): 'Even an Act of Parliament cannot make a freehold estate in land an easement, anymore than it could make two plus two equal to five.' But that fairly reasonable limit on Parliamentary power was subsequently rejected by Lord Justice Scrutton who said (*Taff Vale Railway Co v Cardiff Railway Co*, 1917): 'I respectfully disagree with him, and think that ... it can affect both these statutory results.'

Sometimes the drafting of legislation is so excessively literal it is almost painful. For example, consider the way that Schedules to the Brighton Corporation Act 1931 are defined in that legislation. They manifest what the former High Court Judge, Sir Robert Megarry, describes as the style of pomp and circumstance. The Act could have simply said that the word 'Schedule' appearing in the Act refers to 'a Schedule to this Act' instead, however, what it actually said was:

'The First Schedule' 'the Second Schedule' 'the Third Schedule' 'the Fourth Schedule' 'the Fifth Schedule' 'the Sixth Schedule' 'the Seventh Schedule' 'the Eighth Schedule' 'the Ninth Schedule' 'the Tenth Schedule' 'the Eleventh Schedule' 'the Twelfth Schedule' and 'the Thirteenth Schedule' mean respectively the First Second Third Fourth Fifth Sixth Seventh Eighth Ninth Tenth Eleventh Twelfth and Thirteenth Schedules to this Act.

Not, perhaps, the sort of answer you would expect when asking for directions to the local train station. The real problem comes however, as Sir Robert has observed, when drafting makes something difficult to understand. He cites the Teachers (Compensation) (Advanced Further Education) Regulations 1983, S.I.1983, No 856. They include this passage:

In these Regulations a reference to a Regulation is a reference to a Regulation contained therein, a reference in a Regulation or the Schedule to a paragraph is a reference to a paragraph of that Regulation or the Schedule and a reference in a paragraph to a sub-paragraph is a reference to a sub-paragraph of that paragraph.

Whatever that is, it is not a plainly worded law. Writing clear, unambiguous laws to cover potentially very complicated issues is a substantial challenge. It is arguably impossible, philosophically, to write any legislation without at some time using language which is ambiguous. It is also very difficult to be prescient. When framing a rule, considerable foresight is required to anticipate all of the ways that people might behave and all the events that might develop in the future. Mr Justice Stephen once observed (*Re Castioni*, 1891) that:

> It is not enough to attain to a degree of precision which a person reading in good faith can understand; but it is necessary to attain if possible to a degree of precision which a person reading in bad faith cannot misunderstand. It is all the better if he cannot pretend to misunderstand it.

The way that the words written in the sections of statutes are interpreted by judges in law courts is very important. It is the law brought to life. Flicking through the music manuscript of an opera, or a concerto, and trying to imagine what it would sound like is a very different experience from sitting in an auditorium and hearing the music played by an orchestra. Judges animate the law in the way that musicians animate a manuscript.

A word or phrase can mean different things, and its precise legal meaning is often only clarified when a court comes to declare its meaning. Take the expression 'public place'. In *David Lewis v Director of Public Prosecutions* (2004), a pub car park (private land) was ruled to be a 'public place', during licensing hours, for the purposes of drink driving law.

Police officers discovered David Lewis driving his vehicle in the car park of the Black Bull pub in Ruislip, Middlesex. He was over the legal alcohol limit. The High Court ruled that it could be assumed, without proof, that a pub car park open to the public was a 'public place'. In 1947, in upholding the drink-driving conviction of a Mr Cartlidge, who had been caught in grounds adjoining the Fox and Hounds near Otley, Yorkshire, the High Court observed in *Elkins v Cartlidge* that a public place was 'a place to which the public have access'.

In other areas of law, however, the phrase 'public place' has been differently interpreted. In *Brannan v Peek* (1947), the High Court decided that the courts should not be confused by 'common parlance', and that a 'public house' was *not* a 'public place'. Mr Brannan was prosecuted under the Street Betting Act 1906 for taking racing bets in the Chesterfield Arms in Derby. The High Court decided that, under the Act, the pub was 'no more a public place than a draper's shop' because the public did not have a right of access to it – the invitation to guests could be withdrawn at any time. Mr Brannan was therefore not guilty of an offence under the 1906 Act.

Another case, *Cooper and others v Shield* (1971), concerned a group of nine thugs accused of using threatening behaviour on the platform of West Kirby station. The court ruled that a station platform was not, as required by the Public Order Act 1936, a 'public place' because it was an integral part of a *building* – the station – and incidents in buildings (apart from public meetings) were beyond the scope of the legislation.

A danger due to the state of the premises

A decision of the Court of Appeal provides a good illustration of how the application of a simple legislative phrase to a simple situation may have to go beyond solicitors and barristers, and even the judgment of a county court judge, before it is settled. The case of *Keown v Coventry Healthcare NHS Trust* (2006) concerned Martyn Keown, an 11-year-old boy who had been climbing the underside of a fire escape at the Gulson Hospital in Coventry when he fell to ground and was injured. The fire escape went to the top of the three-floor building. It was in part of the hospital grounds that were used by the public as a means of going between the streets on either side.

The Occupiers' Liability Act 1984 s. 1(1)(a) says that if someone who is legally a trespasser, like Martyn Keown, is to win damages after being injured on premises then, among other things, there must be a 'danger due to the state of the premises'. The trial judge held that there was such a danger. Those seem like quite clear words but in this case there was a dispute about how far, when you are considering whether there was 'a danger', you are allowed to take into account the way in which people – even trespassers – might use the premises.

The NHS Trust submitted that the fire escape was not *itself* dangerous and that any danger was due to Martyn Keown's activity on the premises and not the state of the premises. Mr Keown's counsel submitted that there *was* danger due to the state of the premises 'as found by' Martyn Keown, since the fire escape was amenable to being climbed from the outside with a consequent risk of harm from falling from a height. He argued that it constituted an inducement to children habitually playing in the grounds of the hospital. It was dangerous because children would be tempted to climb it. The healthcare trust appealed against the county court decision that it was liable for the personal injuries suffered by a trespasser.

The trust won its appeal. Mr Keown was not entitled to damages. The judge had found that Martyn Keown had not only appreciated that there was a risk of falling but also that what he was doing was dangerous and that he should not have been climbing the exterior of the fire escape. In the circumstances, it could not be said that Martyn Keown did not recognise the danger. The risk arose not out of the state of the premises, which were as one would expect them to be, but out of what Martyn Keown chose to do. Therefore, Martyn Keown had *not* suffered injury by reason of any 'danger due to the state of the premises' and did not pass that requirement in s. 1(1)(a) of the 1984 Act.

In his judgment Mr Justice Lewison says:

> [T]here was nothing inherently dangerous about the fire escape. There was no physical defect in it: no element of disrepair or structural deficiency. Nor was there any hidden danger. The only danger arose from the activity of Mr Keown [called 'Mr' as he was 21 when the case came to the Court of Appeal] in choosing to climb up the outside, knowing it was dangerous to do so.

The judges of the Court of Appeal analysed relevant case law before coming to a judgment, and there are some subtle points of reasoning in the judgments. But the decision really turns on the ruling about what the statute's simple words mean when applied to the awful accident outside Gulson Hospital.

THE RULES OF INTERPRETATION

The *principles* according to which statutes are interpreted by judges are sometimes known as the 'rules of statutory interpretation'. Calling them 'rules' can be misleading though because they do not necessarily have to be applied by judges. They are more like guidelines than rules. They are the precepts judges can use when interpreting the meaning of words in a statute. Citizens in general and lawyers' clients in particular need to know how judges will interpret the words of statutes. Knowing the 'rules' that the judges will utilise is therefore very helpful. Such knowledge, however, is not determinative of the issues because there is no way of knowing with confidence which guidelines the judges will use to help them. Applying different rules will produce different results.

According to the traditional theory of the division of powers, the role of the judiciary is simply to apply the law that Parliament has created. This view is, however, simplistic because it ignores the extent to which the judiciary has a measure of discretion and a creative power in the way in which it interprets the legislation that comes before it.

In all legislation, ambiguous words and phrases create uncertainty that can only be resolved by judicial interpretation. That interpretation is a creative process and inevitably involves the judiciary in the process of creating law. The question arises, therefore, as to what techniques judges use to interpret legislation that comes before them, and the usual answer is that they can make use of one of the three primary 'rules' of statutory interpretation and of a variety of other secondary aids to construction.

The three principal 'rules' of statutory interpretation often referred to in older cases are: (a) the literal rule; (b) the golden rule; and (c) the mischief rule. Commonly, the rules are not overtly applied by trial judges or appeal judges. A judgment's method of statutory interpretation is only labelled as, for example, 'using the literal method' by lawyers or academics after it has been published.

THE LITERAL RULE

Under this rule, the judge considers what the legislation *actually* says, rather than considering what it *might mean*. In order to achieve this end, the judge should give words in legislation their literal meaning, that is, their plain, ordinary, everyday meaning, even if the effect of this is to produce what might be considered as an otherwise unjust or undesirable outcome. The 'literal rule' is based on the assumption that the words selected by Parliament to express its intention in passing the legislation were exactly what it wanted to express. As the legislative democratic part of the state, Parliament must be taken to want to effect exactly what it says in its laws. To the extent that judges are permitted to give unobvious or non-literal meanings to the words of Parliamentary law, then the will of Parliament, and thereby of the people, is being contradicted. Lord Diplock once noted (*Duport Steel v Sirs* (1980)):

> where the meaning of the statutory words is plain and unambiguous it is not for the judges to invent fancied ambiguities as an excuse for failing to give effect to its plain meaning because they consider the consequences for doing so would be inexpedient, or even unjust or immoral.

In *Fisher v Bell* (1961), the Restriction of Offensive Weapons Act 1959 made it an offence to 'offer for sale' certain offensive weapons including 'flick-knives'. James Bell, a Bristol shopkeeper, displayed a weapon of this type – an 'Ejector knife 4s' – in his shop window in the Arcade, Broadmead. The Divisional Court held that he could not be convicted because, giving the words in the Act their tight, literal legal meaning, Mr Bell had not 'offered for sale' the knives. In the law of contract, placing something in a shop window is not, technically, an 'offer for sale', it is merely an 'invitation to treat'. It is the customer who, legally, makes an 'offer' to the shop when he proffers money for an item on sale. The position would have been different if the legislative phrase had been 'expose for sale'.

THE GOLDEN RULE

This rule is used when application of the literal rule will result in what appears to the court to be an obviously absurd result. An example of application of the golden rule is *Adler v George* (1964). Under s. 3 of the Official Secrets Act 1920, it was an offence to obstruct HM Forces *in the vicinity of* a prohibited place. Mr Frank Adler had in fact been arrested whilst obstructing such forces *within* such a prohibited place – Marham Royal Air Force Station in Norfolk. The court applied the golden rule to extend the literal wording of the statute to cover the action committed by the defendant. If the literal rule had been applied, it would have entailed the absurdity that someone protesting near the base would be committing an offence while someone protesting in it would not.

THE MISCHIEF RULE

This rule was clearly established in *Heydon's Case* (1584). It gives the court a justification for going behind the actual wording of a statute in order to consider the problem that the particular statute was aimed at remedying. At one level, the mischief rule is clearly the most flexible rule of interpretation, but it is limited to using previous common law to determine what mischief the statute in question was designed to remedy. *Heydon's Case* concerned a dispute about legislation passed under Henry VIII in 1540, and a legal action against Heydon for 'intruding into certain lands, &c. in the county of Devon'. It was stated by the court that it should consider the following four matters:

(a) what was the common law before the passing of the statute?
(b) what was the mischief in the law with which the common law did not adequately deal?
(c) what remedy for that mischief had Parliament intended to provide?
(d) what was the reason for Parliament adopting that remedy?

An example of the use of the mischief rule is found in *Corkery v Carpenter* (1951). On 19 January 1951, Shane Corkery was sentenced to one month's imprisonment for 'being drunk in charge of a bicycle' in public. The law report records that at about 2.45 p.m. one afternoon in Devon, the defendant was drunk and was 'pushing his pedal bicycle along Broad Street, Ilfracombe'. He was subsequently charged under s. 12 of the Licensing Act 1872 with being 'drunk in charge of a carriage', as the legislation made no actual reference to cycles. It is certainly arguable that a cycle is not a carriage, but in any case, the court elected to use the mischief rule to decide the matter. The purpose of the Act was to prevent people from using any form of transport on the public highways whilst in a state of intoxication. The cycle was clearly a form of transport and therefore its user was correctly charged.

Apart from the supposed rules of interpretation considered above, the courts may also make use of certain presumptions. As with all presumptions, these are open to rebuttal. These presumptions include the following:

PRESUMPTION AGAINST PARLIAMENT CHANGING THE LAW

Since Parliament is sovereign, it can, of course, alter the common law by express enactment. But it must be express and explicit. The common law cannot be changed by a mere implication that it should. So, a statute is presumed not to make any change to the common law if it is possible to make an alternative interpretation which maintains the existing common law position. Thus, before the Criminal Evidence Act 1898, a wife was incompetent to give evidence against her husband in a trial. To preserve the absolute sanctity of marriage, she could not be called as a witness no matter what he was accused of doing, and however crucially useful her testimony might be. The 1898 legislation changed the law. It made her competent to give evidence. However, that is as far as it went. So, the House of Lords in *Leach v R* (1912) held that the legislation could not be taken to have made a wife a 'compellable witness' — that is, someone whom the court could order, under threat of punishment, to give evidence. A competent witness (meaning someone who has the capacity to be a witness rather than someone who is a proficient performer) is a different legal category in law from a compellable witness, and the 1898 Act only explicitly moved the wife from being in neither category to being in the first of these categories.

PRESUMPTION AGAINST IMPOSING CRIMINAL LIABILITY WITHOUT FAULT

Crimes are serious wrongs, so it is generally assumed that they cannot be committed by someone who does not have at least some form of guilty mind. This can be a very particular form of guilty mind — like an intention to produce harm — or a more vague form of guilty mind like negligence. In law, the mental element of a crime is known as the *mens rea*. It is part of a longer Latin saying *actus non facit reum nisi mens sit rea* meaning 'an act does not make a person guilty unless his mind is guilty'. The states of mind it includes vary across the different sorts of crime known to the law. They include 'intention' and 'gross negligence'. But there are also crimes that do not require any *mens rea* for there to be a conviction.

It is possible for Acts to create offences — like motoring offences — for which no sort of guilty mind is necessary in order for the defendant to be convicted. But it is right for society to be wary about the number of offences like that, so the courts presume that a statute does not impose criminal liability without the need for proof of mental element unless it specifies explicitly that that is what it is doing. In *Sweet v Parsley* (1970), Stephanie Sweet, the owner of Fries Farm in Gosford and Watereaton in Oxfordshire, was charged, contrary to s. 5(b) of the Dangerous Drugs Act 1965, of being concerned in the management of premises which had been used for the purpose of smoking cannabis. The House of Lords decided that as she did not know her property was being used for that purpose, she could not be guilty of the offence with which she was charged. She was a sub-tenant of a farm who had let it to students but retained a room for her own occasional use. Lord Reid said (1972 13): 'whenever a section is silent as to the *mens rea* there is a presumption that ... we must read in words appropriate to require *mens rea*.'

PRESUMPTION AGAINST RETROSPECTIVE OPERATION

A statute is presumed not to operate retrospectively. It is, however, always open to Parliament to enact such legislation, as it did with the War Damage Act 1965. Property of the British-owned Burmah Oil Company was destroyed in 1942, on the orders of a military commander acting in furtherance of a government 'scorched earth policy'. This was done to prevent the Japanese army from taking the installations intact. In *Burmah Oil Co v Lord Advocate* (1965), the company won a substantial damages claim in the House of Lords, but then the government passed the Act to prevent the company from collecting damages. In principle, this is not different from being convicted of driving a red car last year under legislation passed this year to prohibit such activity. In both cases, the company case, and the car case, law is being retrospectively applied to a situation which, when it occurred, was subject to a different law.

OTHER AIDS TO INTERPRETATION

Other sorts of information can be used by a judge in court to determine the meaning of the words in an Act, and if there is an ambiguity in a word or phrase, to choose the preferred interpretation. These aids come from within the statute itself, and some particular principles of language. Looking at the whole of the statute it is acceptable to presume that a word should be given the same meaning wherever it appears in the same statute.

Ejusdem generis: this is Latin for 'of the same type'. It signifies that where particular words describing a category or genus of persons or things are followed by general words, then, subject to any reasons for not thinking so, the general words will be confined to persons or things of the same class as the particular words. The Betting Act 1853 prohibited the keeping of a 'house, office, room or other place' for betting. In *Powell v Kempton Park Race Course* (1899), the court had to decide whether a place within a racecourse known as Tattersall's Ring was covered by the words 'other place' in the phrase 'house, office, room or other place'. The court decided it did not because the words 'house, office, room' created a *genus* (type) of indoor places within which a racecourse – as it was outdoors – did not fall.

Noscitur a sociis: in Latin this means 'it is known from fellows or allies'. It signifies the principle that meaning of a doubtful word can be ascertained by reference to the meaning of the words associated with it. So in *Pengelley v Bell Punch Co Ltd* (1964), the Factories Act 1961, s. 28, fell to be interpreted. The case arose from an industrial injury suffered by Edward Pengelley at the defendant's factory in Uxbridge, Middlesex. It was held that the word 'floors' within the expression 'floors, steps, stairs, passages and gangways', which the Act required to be kept free from obstruction, could not be applied to a part of the factory floor used for storage rather than passage, as the other words 'steps, stairs, passages and gangways' are all locations designed for human movement.

Expressio unius est exclusio alterius. This is Latin for 'the expression of the one is the exclusion of the other'. This means that the express mention in a document of one or more members, or things, of a particular class may be taken as tacitly excluding others of the same class which are not mentioned. In *R v Inhabitants of Sedgley* (1831) words in the Poor Relief Act 1601 required interpretation. It was held that a section that imposed a poor rate on the occupiers of 'lands', houses, tithes and 'coal mines' did not apply to mines other than coal mines, even though the word 'lands' would normally cover all kinds of mine. Lord Tenterden, the Chief Justice, said (1831: 73):

> I take it to be now established as law, by the several decisions, that the expression of coal mines in the Statute ... has the effect of excluding all other mines, according to the maxim 'expressio unius'.

Generalia specialibus non derogant: in Latin this means 'general provisions cannot derogate from specific provisions'. Its significance was very well encapsulated by Mr Justice Sterling in *Re Smith's estate* when he said (1887: 595):

> where there is an Act of Parliament which deals in a special way with a particular subject-matter, and that is followed by a general Act of Parliament, which deals in a general way with a subject-matter of the prevision legislation, the court ought not to hold that general words in such a general Act of Parliament effect a repeal of the prior and special legislation unless it can find some reference in the general Act to the prior and special legislation.

HUMAN RIGHTS AND INTERPRETING UK LAW

The introduction of the Human Rights Act 1998 has had a significant effect on the English legal system generally. Its impact upon statutory interpretation has been extensive. Section 3 of the Human Rights Act requires all legislation to be read, so far as possible, to give effect to the rights provided under the Convention. This section provides the courts with new and extended powers of interpretation. It also has the potential to invalidate previously accepted interpretations of statutes – which were made, of necessity, without recourse to the European Convention on Human Rights. The Act brings the European Convention into United Kingdom law. An examination of some cases reveals how this power has been used by the courts.

A SEXUAL ORIENTATION CASE

The Rent Act 1977, by Schedule 1 paragraph 2, allows a surviving spouse to succeed to the tenancy of a flat if the other spouse dies. It says:

> 2(1) The surviving spouse (if any) of the original tenant, if residing in the dwelling-house immediately before the death of the original tenant, shall after the death be the statutory tenant if and so long as he or she occupies the dwelling-house as his or her residence.
>
> (2) For the purposes of this paragraph, a person who was living with the original tenant as his or her wife or husband shall be treated as the spouse of the original tenant.

Should the words 'spouse', 'husband' and 'wife' in these paragraphs be interpreted to include only heterosexual survivors, and, if so, why? Why should a man or woman whose life partner was the same sex be treated differently as a rent-payer than they would be treated if their deceased partner had been a different sex? In *Ahmad Raja Ghaidan v Antonio Mendoza* (2004), the House of Lords held that it was possible under the Human Rights Act 1998 s. 3 to interpret the Rent Act provision so that it was compliant with rights in the European Convention on Human Rights 1950. It ruled that it was necessary to depart from an earlier interpretation of the Rent Act provision enunciated in the case of *Fitzpatrick v Sterling Housing Association* (2001). The Rent Act should be interpreted as though the survivor of a homosexual couple living together was the surviving spouse of the original tenant.

In 1983, Mr Hugh Wallwyn-James was granted an oral residential tenancy of a flat in West London. Until his death in 2001 he lived there in a stable and monogamous homosexual relationship with the defendant Mr Juan Godin-Mendoza. After the death of Mr Wallwyn-James the landlord, Mr Ahmad Ghaidan, brought proceedings claiming possession of the flat. The Lords held that the Rent Act provision fell within the ambit of the 'right to respect for a person's home' guaranteed by the European Convention on Human Rights 1950 Article 8. It would be wrong to discriminate between heterosexual and homosexual couples in this context since the distinction on grounds of sexual orientation had no legitimate aim and was made without good reason.

However, in spite of this potential increased power, the House of Lords found itself unable to use s. 3 in *Bellinger v Bellinger* (2003).The case related to the rights of transsexuals and the court found itself unable, or at least unwilling, to interpret s. 11(c) of the Matrimonial Causes Act 1973 in such a way as to allow a male to female transsexual to be treated in law as a female. Nonetheless, the court did issue a 'declaration of incompatibility'. This is an action it can take under the Human Rights Act 1998 where a higher court judges an Act to be incompatible with a relevant part of the European Convention on Human Rights. Sucha declaration does not change UK law but does allow Parliament to change the existing law, if it wishes to, using a 'fast track' method.

THE EUROPEAN CONTEXT

There are two distinct types of law coming from Europe. There is:

(a) The law that comes from the European Union – now a grouping of 27 states, but only six countries when the UK joined with two other countries in 1972; it was then called the European Communities (EC). This is largely an economic entity although it does now have important social and political aspects.

(b) The law that comes from a separate entity with different historical roots: the European Court of Human Rights in Strasbourg. The Court enforces the European Convention on Human Rights and Fundamental Freedoms signed by 10 states in 1950. In the UK, the Human Rights Act 1998 adopts these principles as part of national law.

The use of a 'purposive' interpretation approach by the courts is becoming something of a standard approach since the UK joined the European Union. Continental European legal technique, in both a European Union setting and a European human rights setting, has historically set much store by a purposive approach to interpreting legislation. In this context, the key question for the courts is: what was the purpose of the rule, and the legislation or code of which it is a part?

There are comparisons here with the influence of EU Law. For example in *Pepper v Hart* (1993), the House of Lords abolished the long-established convention that the British courts do not look at *Hansard* (the transcript of everything said in Parliament) to discover the parliamentary intention behind legislation. The case arose from an issue of tax law, and the cases of staff from Malvern College. The Lords ruled that the convention against any reference being allowed to *Hansard* when interpreting statutes should be relaxed so as to permit reference to parliamentary materials where: (1) legislation was ambiguous or obscure or led to absurdity; (2) the material relied upon consisted of one or more statements by a minister or other promoter of the Bill together if necessary with such other parliamentary material as was necessary to understand such statements and their effect; and (3) the statements relied on were clear.

This was influenced by the approach of European law, where it is common to look for the purpose of a law in order to interpret that law and to look for that purpose in the legislative history. The community law doctrine of proportionality is also having a great influence. That doctrine, which is drawn from German administrative law principles, is a tool for judging the lawfulness of administrative action. It amounts to this: excessive means are not to be used to attain permissible objectives.

A good example of this approach can be found in the House of Lords decision in *White v White and Motor Insurance Bureau* (2001). Shortly after midnight, in the early moments of 5 June 1993, Brian White was going to a late-night party. He was a front seat passenger in a Ford Capri. The car was being driven by his brother Shane along a country road a few miles outside Hereford. The car crashed and rolled over violently. Brian was very seriously injured. The accident happened at a quiet time of night, and no other vehicle was involved. Shane's driving was at fault. He lost control of the car coming out of a bend through not driving safely and properly. Shane was at fault in another respect: neither he nor the car was insured. Indeed, he had not passed a driving test and, moreover, he was disqualified from driving. At the time of the accident Brian did not know his brother was unlicensed and, hence, uninsured, but he had known in the past that his brother was driving without a licence. The trial judge, Judge Potter, sitting as a judge of the High Court, said that while it would be going too far to say that Brian knew Shane was uninsured, it 'stands out a mile' that he ought to have known. He ought to have made sure one way or the other, and he made no effort to do so.

Brian tried to get compensation from an organisation, the Motor Insurance Bureau (MIB), which pays compensation in certain circumstances when a blameworthy driver is uninsured. Whether Brian got the compensation or not depended upon the interpretation of the words 'knew or ought to have known' as they appeared in an EEC Council Directive, and an MIB document.

The relevant UK law was made on a template of law from the EU, so some background to this is important. Part of the social and political purpose of the European Union is, for fairness and equality across all member states, to make sure the same main law applies in each separate jurisdiction in matters that affect areas like commerce, trade, industry and companies. European Directives are addressed to one or more member states, and require them to achieve specified results. How that is done by regulations or legislation is a matter for the individual states. This directive was to ensure a uniformity of insurance practice across Europe.

At issue in this case was whether, when he got in the car, Brian 'knew or ought to have known' that his brother was uninsured. If so, then the MIB would not pay. In the event, the Lords used a purposive approach in interpreting the legislation. They looked at what purpose the relevant law was designed to achieve, and, in the light of that, ruled that, in effect, the Motor Insurance Bureau were bound to pay compensation to Brian.

Lord Nicholls stated that when interpreting any document it was always important to identify, if possible, the purpose the provision was intended to achieve. That made it necessary to go to the relevant European Directive, which the English law implemented, on the approximation of the laws of the member states relating to insurance against civil liability in respect of the use of motor vehicles. It was necessary to do so because the purpose of the 1988 MIB agreement had been to give effect to the terms of that Directive. Article 1(4) of the Directive provided for the setting up of bodies in member states to provide compensation for damage or injuries caused by uninsured vehicles. It then stated: 'However, member states may exclude the payment of compensation … in respect of persons who voluntarily entered the vehicle … when the body can prove that they *knew* it was uninsured' [italics added]. What was meant by 'knew' in the context of the Directive? The general rule was that people who suffer loss or injury should get compensation. What the Directive sought to do was to permit countries to exclude from any compensation scheme people who had deliberately or knowingly driven while not insured.

The European Court of Justice had stressed repeatedly in cases that exceptions were to be interpreted narrowly. In other words any phrase that sought to *exclude* a category of person from getting compensation should be given the narrowest, strictest interpretation in order to keep those denied compensation to the smallest number.

Here, a strict and narrow interpretation of what constituted knowledge was reinforced by the subject-matter. Proportionality required that a high degree of personal fault must exist before it would be right for an injured passenger to be deprived of compensation. In its context, knowledge that a driver was uninsured meant primarily possession of information from which the passenger drew the conclusion that the driver was uninsured. Most obviously, that occurred where the driver told the passenger so, but the information might be obtained in many other ways, as where the passenger knew that the driver had not passed his test.

Knowledge of that character was often labelled 'actual knowledge'. There was one category of case so close to actual knowledge that the law generally treated a person as having knowledge. That was where a passenger had information from which he had drawn the conclusion that the driver might well not be insured but had deliberately refrained from asking lest his suspicions should be confirmed – where he had wanted not to know. Such a passenger as much colluded in the use of an uninsured vehicle as one who actually knew. They should be treated alike. The Directive was to be construed accordingly. Lord Nicholls was, however, in no doubt that 'knew' in the Directive did not include what could be described broadly as carelessness or negligence. Typically that would cover the case where the passenger had given no thought to the question of insurance, even though an ordinary prudent passenger, in his position and with his knowledge, would have made inquiries. A passenger who was careless in that way could not be treated as though he *knew* of the absence of insurance. As Lord Denning, Master of the Rolls, had said in *Compania Maritima San Basilio SA v Oceanus Mutual Underwriting Association (Bermuda) Ltd* (1977: 68), negligence in not knowing the truth was not equivalent to knowledge of it. To decide otherwise would be to give a wide, rather than a narrow, interpretation to the exception permitted by the Directive.

The circumstances of Brian White's accident came within that last category of case. The judge had rejected the idea that on the night in question any one of those involved had 'so much as bothered his head about such a matter as insurance'. His finding that Brian ought to have made sure that Shane was insured was no more than a finding of carelessness. Thus the accident fell outside the circumstances in which the Directive permitted a member state to exclude payment of compensation.

The British approach to statutory interpretation will change over time as a result of the Human Rights Act 1998, rather in the way that it has done as a result of the European Communities Act 1972. The tools of construction used in mainland Europe are different from those used in the English courts. In Europe, for example, the 'teleological approach' is concerned with giving the instrument its presumed legislative intent. Teleology is a philosophical term meaning that some things are better understood in terms of their purpose than their cause. This approach to the interpretation of statutes is less concerned with examining the words used in an Act with a dictionary to hand, and more concerned with divining the purpose of the law and deciding upon the meaning of its words in the light of that general purpose.

In modern times the emphasis on identifying the true substance at issue has been seen in diverse areas. In tax law, new techniques have developed to view the substance of a transaction overall rather than to be mesmerised by the form of an isolated step within it. In the area of statutory control of leases, the courts are now keen to prevent any set form of words being used to obscure the reality of the underlying transaction. In the area of contract law there has been a move away from literal and semantic analysis and a greater emphasis on discerning the real intent of the parties.

Having examined how the judges and lawyers interpret legislation we turn in the next chapter to explore how judges and lawyers interpret and apply case law.

4

HOW JUDGES DECIDE CASES

In 1968, Mr Justice Donaldson said that 'judges do not act as computers' into which the law is loaded and out of which comes 'the mathematically correct answer'. Judging cases is more of an art than a science.

The key part of a case for the people involved in it is whether they win or lose. But, from a general viewpoint, in the more important cases, the key part of a case is what it declares to be the law. This manufacture of law from the Bench is sometimes called judicial legislation. Law reports vary considerably in length. Some of the older ones are no longer than one sentence. Many from later times run to over a hundred pages.

TITLES

The first thing to note about cases, before examining how the law is to be distilled from them, is their presentational style. Case names are written in a particular way. For example *Miller v Jackson* (1977). The 'v' in the middle stands for *versus* which is Latin for 'against'. Either side are the names of the parties. The first name is the person or organisation that brought the case. If the case is a civil case, that person is called the 'claimant' (formerly called the 'plaintiff') and the other party is called the defendant.

Where a case concerns a dispute over a will it can be titled *In re* (Latin for 'in the matter of') a person or item, for example, *In re Thompson*, concerning the will of Mr Thompson. Sometimes the name of a ship is used as the title, as *In re Polemis*, although such cases often have a longer title as well, like *Re an Arbitration between Polemis and Furness Withy & Co* (1921). The use of longer Latin phrases in civil law was replaced under the Civil Procedure Rules 1998 by English phrases. However, older case titles still bear the Latin. One common reference is e*x parte*. It means 'from a party or faction' and indicates that an application by one side alone has been made to a court, without the presence of the other. The new phrase to describe such actions is 'without notice' applications. The words *ex parte* can also mean 'on behalf of' and are used in some actions in which the person himself cannot proceed but has to ask the Crown to act: for example, in claiming that a court has acted wrongly as in *R v Bow Street Metropolitan Stipendiary Magistrate ex parte Pinochet Ugarte* (2000).

In a criminal case, the person bringing the case is called the prosecutor, and the other person is called the defendant. If the case is *R v Smith*, the 'R' stands for *Rex* (King) or *Regina* (Queen) and shows that the case is a criminal prosecution being brought by the Crown, i.e. the state. Sometimes, especially important cases are brought by the Attorney-General, the government's chief lawyer, or are prosecuted by the Director of Public Prosecutions, the head of the Crown Prosecution Service, in which case the title will be *Att-Gen v Smith* or *DPP v Smith*. The way cases are referred to, or, to use the technical word, cited by lawyers – the letters and numbers – are decoded for you later in this chapter.

Most types of law report carry a summary of the themes at the top of the report, followed by a note of the main facts of the case, and then a heading marked 'Held' meaning what the court decided. The summary of points and the decision are known as the Headnote. There then follows the judgment of the judge (or judges), and at the bottom of the report is recorded the final outcome of the proceedings.

Most of what goes into the law report of a case is the narrative of the facts, and the legal discussion on which a judgment is based. The legal key to the case is not the actual decision in a case like 'guilty' or 'the defendant is liable to pay compensation'. The key is its *ratio decidendi* – this is Latin for 'the reason for deciding'. This is the legal principle applied to the key facts that led to the judgment. It is an 'extracted distillate' (in the phrase of the former judge John Gray) and usually incorporates a combination of facts found and law applied by the court in a previous case.

RATIO DECIDENDI

Consider the case of *Fardon v Harcourt-Rivington*. It went all the way to the House of Lords (now the Supreme Court) in 1932.

Mr and Mrs Seaward Harcourt-Rivington (Seaward was the man's first name and it was the custom then to refer to a couple using the full name of the husband) of Langham Street, London, left their car outside Selfridges store in Somerset Street, off Oxford Street in London. In their car they left their large Airedale dog while they popped out to a shop. For a reason that could not later be discovered, the dog became excited and started jumping around and barking furiously. It was not thought that the dog was suffering from dehydration or having overheated. The dog pawed the rear glass window. The window pane shattered and a shard of glass flew off and, unfortunately, into the eye of a passer-by, Mr Oliver Fardon of Vivian Avenue, in Wembley, Middlesex. Despite operations to remedy the injury, Mr Fardon eventually had the eye removed. His work as a £7-per-week mechanical draughtsman ceased and he became unemployed. He sued the Harcourt-Rivingtons for damages.

Were the couple liable to pay compensation for the man's lost eye? A High Court jury said yes, and he was awarded £2,000. But this was overturned on appeal to the House of Lords. The House of Lords ruled that people should take care to guard against 'realistic possibilities'. They should only be liable, it said, if they caused others harm by doing something that could be reasonably foreseen as likely to cause harm. We are not liable if we fail to guard against 'fantastic possibilities' that happen to occur. The accident in this case, the judges ruled, was just such a 'fantastic possibility'. The couple therefore did not have to pay compensation. The reason for the decision in this case, the *ratio decidendi*, can therefore be expressed simply as: where harm was caused to a pedestrian by a dog smashing the window of the car that it was in, and where this sort of incident was not reasonably foreseeable, the defendants were not liable.

OBITER DICTUM

In a judicial judgment, any statement of law that is not an essential part of the *ratio decidendi* is, strictly speaking, superfluous; and any such statement is referred to as *obiter dictum* (this is Latin for 'a word said while travelling' or 'a word said along the way', *obiter dicta* in the plural). Although *obiter dicta* statements do not form part of the binding precedent, they are persuasive authority and can be taken into consideration in later cases, if the judge in the later case considers it appropriate to do so.

For example, in the case above about the dog, and the man injured by the shard of glass, one judge said that if you knew your dog had an excitable tendency or went mad in cars then you would be liable if it caused someone harm in a predictable way (not in the freakish broken window scenario) and would have to pay compensation. The judge did not need to rule on that in the dog-and-the-car-window case because the couple did *not* have a dog with a known excitable temperament. His observations were, therefore, made 'by the way' and thus can be referred to as an *obiter dictum*. In a future case involving a dog known by its owners to be excitable, a lawyer for an injured claimant could refer back to the judge's *obiter dictum* in the car-window case and use it as 'persuasive' but not 'binding' authority.

The division of cases into these two distinct parts is a theoretical procedure. Unfortunately, judges do not actually separate their judgments into the two clearly defined categories and it is up to the person reading the case to determine what the *ratio* is. In some cases, this is no easy matter, and it may be made even more difficult in cases where there are three or five judges and where each of the judges delivers their own lengthy judgment so there is no clear single *ratio* for the decision. It is possible for a case to have several (in the plural) *rationes decidendi*. In some cases it may be difficult to ascertain precisely the *ratio* of the case and to distinguish the *ratio* from the *obiter dicta*.

Consider *Barnett v Chelsea and Kensington Hospital Management Committee* (1968). The full description of what happened in this case would run to many pages. This, though, was the basic story.

William Patrick Barnett was employed as a night watchman at the hall of residence at the Chelsea College of Sciences and Technology in London. On 31 December 1965, following celebrations with some friends while at the hall of residence, he had to take his friend, who had become injured in an attack, to the hospital. After they returned they all drank some tea and after a while they all began vomiting violently. They returned to the hospital and recounted their symptoms, including continuous vomiting and cramp. The nurse telephoned the casualty officer, a doctor, to tell him of the men's complaint.

The casualty officer, who was himself unwell, did not see them but said that they should go home and call their own doctors. The men went away and Mr Barnett died on the afternoon of 1 January 1966 from what was later found to be arsenical poisoning. The coroner later recorded a verdict of 'murder by a person or persons unknown'. However, even if Mr Barnett had been admitted to hospital, instead of being told to go home, when he arrived at about 8 a.m. on January 1st, it was still too late then for him to have been saved because the arsenic he had ingested at 5 a.m. could not have been counteracted within the time it would have taken (from 8 a.m.) to get him into a bed, give him the appropriate tests, get the results and give the treatment.

In this case, in which the dead man's widow was suing the hospital, the High Court decided that the defendant hospital management committee was *not* liable to pay damages to the deceased's wife and children. From a legal point of view, the important thing is the extraction of the principle on which this decision is based.

The name, age and sex of the victim were irrelevant because the law would apply just the same if any of these data were different. The location of the case is irrelevant because the same law would apply in Leeds as applied in London. The reason the case was decided as it was, was that although the doctor was negligent in not seeing the patient, the death of the victim was not the result of that negligence. Even had the doctor seen the patient, he would inevitably have died because of the stage of his poisoning when he went to the hospital. Accordingly, the hospital was not liable. The hospital *did* owe a duty of care towards the patient, and it *was* in breach of that duty of care when its employee, the doctor, did not check the patient. But the breach of duty could not be said to be the cause of the victim's death. So, in future cases, the relevant law to guide us is that: if a defendant owes a duty of care to another, and is in breach of that duty, he will only be liable if the breach was the cause of the victim's injury, loss or death.

The *ratio* in the Barnett case can be expressed as follows:

> In failing to see and examine the deceased, and in failing to admit him to hospital and treat him, the hospital's casualty officer was negligent but the claimant had not discharged the onus of proving that the deceased's death was caused by the negligence (or, if the onus was on the hospital to show that Mr Barnett's death was not due to its negligence, they had done that) so the claimant's claim failed.

OVERRULING

Within the system of precedent, decisions in major cases gain increased authority with the passage of time. As a consequence, courts tend to be reluctant to overrule long-standing authorities even though they may no longer accurately reflect contemporary practices or morals. While old precepts are not often good in dentistry or computer science, they are sometimes seen that way in law.

In addition to the desire to maintain a high degree of certainty and predictability in the law, another reason for judicial reluctance to overrule old decisions is that overruling operates retrospectively so that the law being overruled is held never to have been the real law. If the House of Lords in 2008 says that a 1998 Court of Appeal statement of the law was incorrect, then, technically, what the 2008 judges rule is the law represents *what it has always been*, from before 1998 and after 2008.

In *Kleinwort Benson Ltd v Lincoln City Council* (1998) the House of Lords overruled various earlier decisions and ruled that, subject to some specific defences, the law should now recognise that there was a general right to recover money paid under a mistake, whether of fact or law. Although they are sometimes necessary, the trouble with this sort of decision is that they apply backwards into the past in a way that legislation rarely does. Lord Goff stated (1998: 537) that:

> the law as declared by the judge is the law applicable not only at the date of the decision but at the date of the events which are the subject

of the case before him, and of the events of other cases *in pari materia* [Latin for 'in like material', i.e. of equal relevance] which may thereafter come before the courts.

The freedom of higher courts to overrule earlier lower courts (or even themselves sometimes) is an essential part of how a system of law must operate if it is to be living law. The courts have the capacity for pruning withered principles, and cultivating gradual organic growth in the law.

DISTINGUISHING

In comparison to the mechanism of overruling which is rarely used, the main device for avoiding binding precedents is that of distinguishing. As has been previously stated, the *ratio decidendi* of any case is an abstraction from, and is based upon, the material facts of the case. This opens up the possibility that a court may regard the facts of the case before it as significantly different from the facts of a cited precedent and thus it may not find itself bound to follow that precedent. Judges use the device of distinguishing where, for some reason, they are unwilling to follow a particular precedent. The law reports provide many examples of strained distinctions where a court has quite evidently not wanted to follow an authority that it would otherwise have been bound by.

Lawyers and judges are always making fine distinctions. If a lawyer is ever faced with a case precedent from an authoritative law court which does not favour his or her client, then the only way around it is to try to put the current case outside the scope of the precedent.

For example, in law an agreement becomes an enforceable contract if, among other things, a formal *offer* is subject to a formal *acceptance*. This was clearly established in precedent when *Pharmaceutical Society of Great Britain v Boots Cash Chemists (Southern Ltd)* 1953 came to be decided. The chemist shop had been accused by the Pharmaceutical Society of selling certain prescription medicines to the public without the supervision of a registered pharmacist as required under the Pharmacy and Poisons Act. On 13 April 1951, two people had gone in Boots at 73 Burnt Oak Broadway in Edgware, London, and bought, respectively, a medicine containing a tiny amount of strychnine, and Famel syrup which contained codeine. These were products required by law to be sold under the supervision of a registered pharmacist. Were the sales made under such supervision?

This charge depended upon there being a *sale* completed when a customer in Boots put a prescribed medicine that was 'offered' on a shelf into his shopping basket, thereby accepting the offer. The offer consummated by the acceptance would seal the contract and effect a sale. If that took place when the shopper put an item in his or her basket, then it would be an unlawful sale because there was no pharmacist supervising the action at that point.

It was argued by lawyers for Boots that this scenario was distinguishable from earlier 'offer and acceptance' cases because the goods on the shelf of the store were *not* offers but merely 'invitations to treat'. It was the customer who, if he took an item to the checkout, was making an offer, and the store that might accept the offer if it rang it up on the till. So the contract was concluded not when the customer put the item in his basket but at the cash till – and there *was* a registered pharmacist near the till so the sale was under his supervision. That argument was accepted by the court, so Boots were not guilty of any offence.

JUDICIAL DEVELOPMENT OF THE LAW

The law relating to psychiatric harm provides a good example of the way that case law has been developed by judicial ingenuity to keep pace with social changes. In what circumstances can someone who has suffered psychiatric injury as a result of having witnessed a terrible accident successfully sue the person whose negligence has caused the accident?

The leading case on recovery of compensation in such circumstances is *Alcock v Chief Constable of South Yorkshire Police* (1991), which arose from the Hillsborough Stadium disaster. At the FA Cup semi-final match at Hillsborough Stadium in Sheffield between Nottingham Forest and Liverpool in April 1989, 96 people were killed and over 400 physically injured in a crush which developed owing to poor crowd control by the police. The Chief Constable admitted liability towards those physically harmed. Many more people variously related to, or connected with, the dead and injured suffered psychiatric illness resulting from the shock of witnessing the event, seeing it on television or identifying the bodies.

Sixteen claims were heard at first instance, of which 10 succeeded in 1991. Mr Justice Hidden held that brothers and sisters, as well as parents and spouses, could sue, but that grandfathers, uncles, brothers-in-law, fiancées and friends could not. He also decided that seeing the scene on television was equivalent to being at the scene itself.

In 1991, the Court of Appeal dismissed all the claims on the ground that, apart from rescuers, only parents and spouses could claim and that 'a perception through the broadcast of selective images accompanied by a commentary is not such as to satisfy the proximity test'. Ten claimants then appealed unsuccessfully to the House of Lords.

Where was the line to be drawn between sufferers of psychiatric harm who could sue those responsible for the disaster and those who could not? The House of Lords refused to prescribe rigid categories of the potential claimants in nervous shock claims. They ruled that there must generally be a close and intimate relationship between the claimant and the primary victim (for example, in the Hillsborough setting, someone who was crushed or asphyxiated) of the sort generally enjoyed by spouses and parents and children. The House of Lords ruled that siblings and other more remote relatives would normally fall outside such a relationship in the absence of special factors. But, for example, a grandmother who had brought up a grandchild since infancy might qualify. Therefore, claims by brothers, sisters and brothers-in-laws failed in *Alcock*, while the claim on the part of a fiancée was allowed. One of the judges, Lord Ackner, suggested that in cases of exceptional horror where even a reasonably strong-nerved individual might suffer shock-induced psychiatric injury, then a bystander unrelated to the victim might recover damages.

The Lords went on to rule that a degree of proximity in time and space between the claimant and the accident is required. The claimant must therefore either actually be at the accident itself and witness it or come on the aftermath in a very short period of time. Identifying a relation several hours after death was not sufficient to pass the legal test. Witnessing the accident via the medium of television will not generally be enough.

Parents who watched the Hillsborough disaster on television had their claims rejected. This is because television pictures would not normally be equated with actual sight or hearing at the event or its aftermath. Two of the Lords, Lord Keith and Lord Oliver, did, however, recognise that there might be exceptional cases where simultaneous broadcasts of a disaster were equivalent to a personal presence at the accident. In the Court of Appeal, Lord Justice Nolan gave the example of a balloon carrying children at some live broadcast event suddenly bursting into flames.

The harm for which the person sues, the psychiatric illness, must be shown to result from the trauma of the event or its immediate aftermath. Psychiatric illness resulting from being informed of a loved one's death, however shocking the circumstances, is not recoverable. The approach taken by the House of Lords in *Alcock* is a very pragmatic one. They rejected the simple approach based on strict categories of those who could and could not recover and in what circumstances. In his judgment, Lord Keith said:

> as regards the class of person to whom a duty may be owed to take reasonable care to avoid inflicting psychiatric illness through nervous shock sustained by reason of physical injury or peril to another, I think it is sufficient that reasonable foreseeability should be the guide. I would not seek to limit the class by reference to particular relationships such as husband and wife or parent and child. The kinds of relationship which may involve close ties of love and affection are numerous, and it is the existence of such ties which leads to mental disturbance when the loved one suffers a catastrophe. They may be present in family relationships or those of close friendship, and may be stronger in the case of engaged couples than in that of persons who have been married to each other for many years.

He went on to say that the closeness of any given emotional tie would need to be proved by a nervous shock claimant although it could be presumed in appropriate cases (e.g. between long-standing life partners). The case of a bystander unconnected with the victim of an accident is more difficult. Psychiatric injury to him or her is not, ordinarily, within the range of 'reasonable foreseeability' although it might be provable if such a person was very close to a particularly horrific incident.

Thus, the *ratio decidendi* of this case, while being one which is reasonably clear, is one nevertheless whose precise application in future cases is difficult to predict. In a subsequent case, *McFarlane v EE Caledonia Ltd* (1994), the Court of Appeal had to apply the general principle expounded by the Lords in *Alcock*. In this case, the claimant, Francis McFarlane, witnessed the destruction of a North Sea oil rig (the Piper Alpha) from aboard a support vessel which had been involved in attempts to rescue survivors of the explosion which tore apart the rig. The claimant was not himself involved directly in the rescue effort and was far enough away from the burning rig to avoid any personal danger to himself. Even so, the events which he witnessed were horrific almost beyond imagining. He had to watch people in agony burning to death as the rig was devastated by fire and explosions. Although technically a 'bystander' to the incident because he was neither a relative of any of the primary victims nor a rescuer, he does seem to fit within the last category of possible claimants described above by Lord Keith. His case, though, was rejected by the Court of Appeal, which suggested that practical and policy reasons militated against allowing him to recover. Lord Justice Stuart-Smith said (1994: 14):

> In my judgment both as a matter of principle and policy the court should not extend the duty to those who are mere bystanders or witnesses of horrific events unless there is a sufficient degree of proximity, which requires both nearness in time and place and a close relationship of love and affection between plaintiff and victim.

In *Henry White and others v Chief Constable of South Yorkshire and Others* (1998), the House of Lords decided that four police officers who were on duty at Hillsborough on the day of the disaster in 1989 which was the subject of the earlier *Alcock* case could not recover damages (as employees or rescuers) for psychiatric injury suffered as a result of tending victims of an incident caused by their employer's negligence. It was admitted by the Chief Constable that the events were caused by the negligence of the police in allowing the over-crowding of two spectator pens. The question was how far compensation should go for alleged psychological injury. The four police officers had actively helped to deal with the human consequences of the tragedy and as a result suffered from post-traumatic stress disorder. Counsel for the police officers argued there was no justi-fication for regarding physical and psychiatric injury as different kinds of damage. They also argued the case on conventional employer's liability principles as well as on the ground that they were rescuers.

In a decision that seems distinctly mindful of social policy (as opposed to mechanical application of the existing rules), the House of Lords ruled, by a majority of three to two, that a recognition of the claims would have substantially expanded the existing categories in which compensation could be recovered for pure psychiatric harm and would have sat uneasily with the denial of the claims of bereaved relatives by the decision of the House of Lords in *Alcock v Chief Constable of South Yorkshire Police*.

DISSENTING JUDGMENTS

In *Henry White and others v Chief Constable of South Yorkshire and Others* (1998), Lords Griffiths and Goff delivered dissenting judgments – or Opinions, as House of Lords judges' judgments are properly termed. They were broadly in favour of the claimants succeeding as rescuers. Although their Opinions were judgments that would have allowed the claimants to succeed, in fact they had no effect in that case because the preponderant opinion – the majority of three law lords – decided against the claimants.

Judges deliver judgments dissenting (*dissentiente*) from that of the majority of judges when their analysis of the law is different from that of their fellow judges. It comes as a surprise to some people that it is not only lawyers who have different understandings of what the same law means; judges also might have divergent opinions. Dissenting opinions are sometimes adopted later by a higher court or by Parliament to represent the law. In an American case, Justice Clarkson said this before delivering his dissent in *Oliver v City of Raleigh* (1937: 857):

> In those after years when this case, elevated to high authority by the cold finality of the printed page, is quoted with the customary 'It has been said' perchance another court will say, 'Mayhaps the potter's hand trembled at the wheel.' Possibly when that moment comes these words may give the court a chance to say, 'Yea, and a workman standing hard by saw the vase as it was cracked.'

Lord Denning became known for his strongly argued dissents in cases, several of which subsequently became law, such as that concerned with the liability for negligent misstatements. In his book *The Discipline of Law*, Denning recounts (1979: 287) some of the dissenting judgments he delivered which 'led to decisions by the Lords which might never have taken place except for my dissenting from previous precedents'.

LAW REPORTING

Precedents cannot be cited to a judge by lawyers if there is not a good record of all the earlier cases and how they were decided. Thus the operation of binding precedent relies on the existence of an extensive reporting service to provide access to previous judicial decisions.

The professionalism and reliability of the doctrine of precedent, therefore, developed in tandem with the development of law reporting. The earliest reports of particular cases appeared between 1275 and 1535 in what are known as The Year Books.

Publication of the private reports was slow and expensive. This situation was at last remedied by the establishment of the Council for Law Reporting in 1865, subsequently registered as a corporate body in 1870 under the name of the Incorporated Council of Law Reporting for England and Wales. The council was established under the auspices of the Inns of Court and the Law Society with the aim of producing quicker, cheaper and more accurate reports than had been produced previously.

The Law Reports are still produced by the Incorporated Council of Law Reporting. They have the distinct advantage of containing summaries of counsels' arguments and, perhaps even more importantly, they are subject to revision by the judges in the case before they are published.

In line with the ongoing modernisation of the whole legal system the way in which cases are to be cited has been changed. Thus since January 2001 a new neutral system was introduced, and cases in the various courts are now cited ('EW' means England and Wales) as follows:

Court of Appeal (Civil Division)   [year] EWCA Civ case no.

Court of Appeal (Criminal Division) [year] EWCA Crim case no.

High Court: Queens Bench Division	[year] EWHC case no. (QB)
Chancery Division	[year] EWHC case no. (Ch)
Patents Court	[year] EWHC case no. (Pat)
Queen's Bench Division	[year] EWHC case no. (QB)
Administrative Court	[year] EWHC case no. (Admin)
Commercial Court	[year] EWHC case no. (Comm)
Admiralty Court	[year] EWHC case no. (Admlty)
Technology & Construction Court	[year] EWHC case no. (TCC)
Family Division	[year] EWHC case no. (Fam)

Within the individual case, the paragraphs of each judgment are numbered consecutively, and where there is more than one judgment the numbering of the paragraphs carries on sequentially. Thus, for example, the decision in *Alcock* was applied in the later case of *Atkinson & Anor v Seghal* (2003). This decided that the immediate aftermath of a fatal road accident in which the claimant's daughter was killed extended from the moment of the accident until the moment the claimant left the mortuary. The civil trial judge had artificially separated the mortuary visit, which was not merely to identify the body but also to complete the story so far as the claimant was concerned. The defendant could be liable on the basis of what was seen at the mortuary. The neutral citation of the case is [2003] EWCA Civ 697. This case was decided in 2003 in the England and Wales Court of Appeal, Civil Division, and its case number is 697. The neutral reports do not have page numbers.

The case is also reported at LTL 21/3/2003, (2003) Lloyd's Rep Med 285, and (2004) 78 BMLR 22. If ever you need information about what the initials of a report stand for (LTL is Lawtel Transcripts, Lloyds Rep Med is Lloyds Law Reports Medical, and BMLR is Butterworths Medico-Legal Reports) a good source is the Cardiff Legal Abbreviations website.

ELECTRONIC LAW

As in most other fields, the growth of information technology has revolutionised law reporting and searching for legal reports and regulations. Many of the law reports mentioned above are both available on CD-ROM and on the internet or on databases such as Justis, Lawtel, Lexis-Nexis, Wetslaw UK amongst others.

If you are ever mystified by a legal citation – the letters and numbers after the name of a case – you need to look at a list of legal abbreviations. The easiest way to get a good list of abbreviations is to visit the website of the British Academy: britac.ac.uk then press the Law option. When the Law page appears, look down the list and click Legal Abbreviations (UK).

JUDGING THE SYSTEM OF PRECEDENT

For the legal system itself, and, more generally for society, the doctrine of precedent carries various advantages and disadvantages.

The advantages of the system include consistency, certainty, efficiency and flexibility. Consistency in approach flows from the fact that 'like cases are decided on a like basis' and are not subject to the whim of the individual judge deciding the case in question. This aspect of formal justice is important in justifying the decisions taken in particular cases. Certainty of what the law is, or something akin to certainty, is enjoyed because lawyers and their clients are able, by looking at past decisions, to predict what the likely answer is to any legal question. So, once a legal rule has been established in one case, individuals can orient their behaviour with regard to that rule relatively secure in the knowledge that it will not be changed by some later court.

Efficiency is promoted because the doctrine of precedent saves the time of the judiciary, lawyers and their clients as similar cases do not have to be repeatedly re-argued before the courts. In respect of potential litigants, it saves them money in court expenses because they can apply to their lawyer for guidance as to how their particular case is likely to be decided in the light of previous cases on the same or similar points. Additionally, some flexibility is built into the system because the discretionary judicial use of overruling, distinguishing, and creative development of the law mean that it should be very rare when a judge has to make a manifestly unfair ruling on no better basis than that such is the inescapable dictate of the law. As Lord Esher once noted in *Emmens v Pottle* (1885: 357): 'Any proposition the result of which would be to show that the common law of England is wholly unreasonable and unjust, cannot be part of the common law of England.'

The disadvantages of the doctrine of precedent include aspects of uncertainty, fixity and unconstitutionality that it can bring to the legal system. They arise from the same facts that generated the advantages. This is so when many things are evaluated: a small, light car might be easy to manoeuvre and to park, and might consume relatively little fuel but it might be less strong and safe than a larger car, and hold fewer people. The uncertainty of the system of precedent comes from the fact that any certainty afforded by the doctrine of *stare decisis* (let the decision stand, i.e. the previous decision should determine the current case) is undermined by the huge number of cases that have been reported and can be cited as authorities. Certainty cannot come from a sea bobbing with so many relevant decisions. With so many rules and slightly different interpretations of them in thousands of cases, it is not always easy to see which interpretation a court will give the law in your case. This uncertainty is increased by the ability of the judiciary to select from what is often a wide range of precedents, and to distinguish earlier cases on their facts where an earlier case if followed would lead to a result unjust in the view of the judge.

The fixity of law promoted by the doctrine of precedent can sometimes be socially disadvantageous. The law in relation to any particular area may become solidified on the basis of an unjust precedent with the consequence that previous injustices are perpetuated. An example of this is the long delay before the courts were willing to change the law and say that marital rape was a crime. Since the 1970s, arguments had been put to the courts on behalf of women raped by their husbands but the law was only amended by the House of Lords in 1992. Another arguable disadvantage flowing from the system of precedent is that it can entail unconstitutional consequences. This refers to the fact that the judiciary might arguably be overstepping their theoretical constitutional role by actually making law rather than restricting themselves to the role of simply applying it. If they are not elected as law-makers then why should they be allowed to make law? Judges are supposed only to make law interstitially – in the intervening spaces between rules. By filling in detail in applying the law, they make new smaller rules. In truth, though, as we have seen, judges can innovate quite substantially.

Now that we have explored how judges decide cases according to UK legislation and cases, we move on in the next chapter to look at European law and how it applies to the UK.

5

THE EUROPEAN UNION

INTRODUCTION

It is unrealistic and indeed impossible for anyone looking to gain an understanding of English law to ignore the UK's membership of the European Union (EU). What makes this even more vital is that the generally antagonistic approach adopted to the EU in the UK press, and by a substantial number of politicians of diverse political views, has meant that many people in the UK approach the whole idea of the EU, and its law and regulations, with a guarded reserve, if not a fully articulated hostility. The purpose of this chapter is to provide some essential background information about the structure and law of the EU in order, hopefully, to allow a more informed assessment of that institution. At the outset, it is essential to distinguish between the two different courts that operate within the European context: the European Court of Justice (ECJ), which is the court of the EU, sitting in Luxembourg; and the European Court of Human Rights (ECtHR), which deals with cases relating to the European Convention on Human Rights (ECHR) and sits in Strasbourg. Some politicians have been known wilfully to conflate, or at least confuse, the two courts. We explain the work of the ECtHR in the next chapter.

THE DEVELOPMENT OF THE EUROPEAN UNION

The long-term process leading to the, as yet still to be attained, establishment of an integrated EU was a response to two factors:

the disasters of the Second World War; and the emergence of the Soviet Bloc in Eastern Europe. The aim was to link the separate European countries, particularly France and Germany, together in such a manner as to prevent the outbreak of future, armed hostilities. The first step in this process was the establishment of a European Coal and Steel Community. The next step towards integration was the formation of the *European Economic Community* (EEC) under the *Treaty of Rome* in 1957. The UK eventually joined the original six members of the EEC in 1973, after previously having been rebuffed by the French President Charles de Gaulle.

The Treaty of Rome was subsequently amended in the further pursuit of integration as the Community expanded. Thus, the *Single European Act* (SEA) 1986 established a single economic market within the EC and widened the use of majority voting in the Council of Ministers. The *Maastricht Treaty* further accelerated the move towards a federal European supranational state, in the extent to which it recognised Europe as a social and political – as well as an economic – community. Previous Conservative governments of the UK resisted the emergence of the EU as anything other than an economic market and objected to, and declined to adopt, various provisions aimed at social, as opposed to economic, affairs. Thus, the UK was able to opt out of the Social Chapter of the Treaty of Maastricht. The New Labour administration in the UK, newly elected in 1997, had no such reservations and, as a consequence, as the UK's dissent had gone, the *Treaty of Amsterdam* of that year incorporated the European Social Chapter into the EU Treaty.

As the establishment of the single market within the European Community progressed, it was suggested that its operation would be greatly facilitated by the adoption of a common currency, or at least a more closely integrated monetary system. Thus, in 1979, the European Monetary System (EMS) was established, under which individual national currencies were valued against a nominal currency called the ECU and allocated a fixed rate within which they were allowed to fluctuate to a limited extent. Britain was a member of the EMS until 1992, when financial speculation against the pound forced its withdrawal. Nonetheless, other members of the EU continued to pursue the policy of monetary union, now entitled European Monetary Union (EMU), and January 1999 saw the installation of the new European currency, the Euro, which has now replaced national currencies within what is now known as the Eurozone. The UK did not join the EMU at its inception and there is little chance that membership will appear on the political agenda for the foreseeable future, especially given the financial crisis that is enveloping many of the EMU states, particularly those on the periphery of the EU.

In December 2000 the European Council met in Nice in the south of France. The Council consists of the heads of state or government of the member countries of the EU, and is the body charged with the power to make amendments to EU treaties (see below). The purpose of the meeting was to prepare the Union for expansion from its then 15 to 25 members by the year 2004, and so to its current 27 members.

Subsequently in February 2002 a *Convention on the Future of Europe* was set up to consider the establishment of a constitution for the European Union. The Convention, which sat under the presidency of the former President of France, Valéry Giscard d'Estaing, produced a draft constitution, which it was hoped would provide a more simple, streamlined and transparent procedure for internal decision-making within the Union and enhance its profile on the world stage. Among the proposals for the new constitution were the following:

- the establishment of a new office of President of the European Union;
- the appointment of a EU foreign minister;
- the shift to a two-tier Commission;
- fewer national vetoes;
- increased power for the European Parliament;
- simplified voting power;
- the establishment of a EU defence force by 'core members';
- the establishment of a charter of fundamental rights.

In the months of May and June 2005 the move towards the European Constitution came to a juddering halt when first the French and then the Dutch electorates voted against its implementation. Such a signal failure meant that it was not necessary for the UK government to conduct a referendum on the proposed constitution as it had promised. However, as with most EU initiatives, the new constitution did not disappear and re-emerged as the *Treaty of Lisbon*, signed by all the members in December 2007.

The Lisbon Treaty gave rise to much ill-feeling in many states for the reason that it incorporated most of the proposals originally contained in the previously rejected constitutional proposal. In legal form, the Lisbon Treaty merely amended the existing treaties, rather than replacing them as the previous constitution had proposed. In practical terms, however, all the essential changes that would have been delivered by the constitution were contained in the treaty – a fact widely recognised by some EU leaders, though not by the UK, where the government declined to hold a referendum on the treaty on the basis of the, not totally convincing, suggestion that the treaty was simply an amendment and a tidying up measure and consequently did not need the confirmation of a referendum in the way necessary and promised for the constitution.

The necessary alterations to the fundamental treaties governing the EU, brought about by the Lisbon Treaty, were published at the end of March 2010 in the form of: an updated *Treaty on European Union* (TEU), a newly named *Treaty on the Functioning of the European Union* (TFEU) (formerly the *Treaty Establishing the European Community*) together with the *Charter of Fundamental Rights of the European Union* (CFREU).

FUNDAMENTAL TREATIES OF THE EUROPEAN UNION

THE TREATY ON EUROPEAN UNION (TEU)

The text of the treaty is divided into six parts as follows, with reference to some of the most important specific provisons.

Article 1 states that '*the Union shall replace and succeed the European Community*'. This provision means that the previous confusion between when it was more appropriate to refer to EC rather than the EU has been removed and that it is now correct under all circumstances to refer to the EU. Article 47 provides further that the EU has legal personality, which means that the EU, as well as its constituent members, will be able to be a full member of the Council of Europe.

Article 3 then states the aims of the EU in very general terms as follows:

- the promotion of peace, its values and the well-being of its peoples;
- the assurance of freedom of movement of persons without internal frontiers but with controlled external borders;
- the creation of an internal market ... aiming at full employment and social progress, and a high level of protection and improvement of the quality of the environment;
- the establishment of an economic and monetary union whose currency is the euro; the promotion of its values, while contributing to the eradication of poverty and observing human rights and respecting the charter of the United Nations;
- the sixth requires that the EU pursues its objectives by 'appropriate means'.

Article 6 binds the EU to the Charter of Fundamental Rights of the European Union and the European Convention on Human Rights.

Article 9 establishes the equality of EU citizens and that every national of a member state shall be a citizen of the Union. However, it makes clear that citizenship of the Union is *additional to* and does *not replace* national citizenship.

Article 13 establishes the institutions in the following order and under the following names (except for the ECB these will be considered in detail below):

- the European Parliament,
- the European Council,
- the Council,
- the European Commission,
- the Court of Justice of the European Union,
- the European Central Bank,
- the Court of Auditors.

Article 15 establishes the President of the European Council.
Article 18 the High Representative of the Union for Foreign Affairs and Security Policy

Articles 21 & 46 relate to the establishment and operation of a common EU foreign policy including:

- compliance with the UN charter, promoting global trade, humanitarian support and global governance;
- establishment of the European External Action Service, which will function as the EU's foreign ministry and diplomatic service;
- the furtherance of military cooperation including mutual defence.

THE TREATY ON THE FUNCTIONING OF THE EUROPEAN UNION (TFEU)

This document, going back through several iterations to the original Treaty of Rome, contains the detail of the structure and operation of the European Union.

Article 2 of this treaty provides that:

> When the Treaties confer on the Union exclusive competence in a specific area, only the Union may legislate and adopt legally binding acts, the Member States being able to do so themselves only if so empowered by the Union or for the implementation of Union acts.

Article 3 specifies that the Union shall have exclusive competence in the following areas:

(a) customs union;
(b) the establishing of the competition rules necessary for the functioning of the internal market;
(c) monetary policy for the member states whose currency is the euro;
(d) the conservation of marine biological resources under the common fisheries policy;
(e) common commercial policy.

Article 3 provides that the Union shall also have exclusive competence for the conclusion of an international agreement when its conclusion is provided for in a legislative act of the Union or is necessary to enable the Union to exercise its internal competence, or in so far as its conclusion may affect common rules or alter their scope.

The provision of specific articles will be considered below.

THE CHARTER OF FUNDAMENTAL RIGHTS OF THE EUROPEAN UNION (CFREU)

The Charter contains 54 articles divided into seven titles. The first six titles deal with substantive rights relating to:

- *dignity*, including the right to life and the prohibition of torture and inhuman or degrading treatment or punishment;
- *freedom*, including the right to liberty and security of person, the right to engage in work and the freedom to conduct a business;
- *equality*, including equality before the law, and the right not to be discriminated against;
- *solidarity*, which emphasises workers' rights to fair working conditions, protection against unjustified dismissal, information and consultation within the undertaking, together with the right to engage in collective bargaining and to engage in industrial action;
- *citizens' rights*, including the right to vote and to stand as a candidate at elections; and finally
- *justice*, which includes the right to a fair trial, the presumption of innocence, and the right of defence.

Many member states, including the UK, have negotiated opt-outs of some of the provisions of the Charter.

PARLIAMENTARY SOVEREIGNTY, EUROPEAN UNION LAW AND THE COURTS

The doctrine of parliamentary sovereignty is one of the cornerstones of the UK constitution. One aspect of the doctrine is that, as long as the appropriate procedures are followed, Parliament is free to make such law as it determines. The corollary of that is that no current Parliament can bind the discretion of a later Parliament to make law as it wishes. The role of the court is merely to interpret the law made by Parliament. Each of these constitutional principles is revealed as problematic in relation to the UK's membership of the EU and the relationship of domestic and EU law.

Before the UK joined the EU, its law was just as foreign as law made under any other jurisdiction. On joining the EU, however, the UK and its citizens accepted, and became subject to, EU law.

This subjection to European law remains the case even where the parties to any transaction are themselves both UK subjects. In other words, in areas where it is applicable, *European law supersedes any existing UK law to the contrary*. The European Communities Act (ECA) 1972 gave legal effect to the UK's membership of the EEC, and its subjection to all existing and future Community/Union law was expressly stated in s. 2(1), which provides that:

> All such rights, powers, liabilities, obligations and restrictions from time to time created or arising by or under the Treaties, and all such remedies and procedures from time to time provided for by or under the Treaties, as in accordance with the Treaties *are without further enactment to be given legal effect or used in the UK* shall be recognised and available in law, and be enforced, allowed and followed accordingly.
>
> [emphasis added]

An example of EU law invalidating the operation of UK legislation can be found in the *Factortame* cases. The Common Fisheries Policy established by the EEC had placed limits on the amount of fish that any member country's fishing fleet was permitted to catch. In order to gain access to British fish stocks and quotas, Spanish fishing boat owners formed British companies and re-registered their boats as British. In order to prevent what it saw as an abuse and an encroachment on the rights of indigenous fishermen, the British government introduced the Merchant Shipping Act 1988, which provided that any fishing company seeking to register as British would have to have its principal place of business in the UK and at least 75 per cent of its shareholders would have to be British nationals. This effectively debarred the Spanish boats from taking up any of the British fishing quota. Some 95 Spanish boat owners applied to the British courts for judicial review of the Merchant Shipping Act 1988 on the basis that it was contrary to Community law.

The High Court decided to refer the question of the legality of the legislation to the ECJ under Article 267 of the Treaty on the Functioning of the European Union (TFEU), but in the meantime granted interim relief, in the form of an injunction disapplying the operation of the legislation to the fishermen. On appeal, the Court of Appeal removed the injunction, a decision that was confirmed by the House of Lords. However, the House of Lords referred the question of the relationship of Community law and contrary domestic law to the ECJ. Effectively, they were asking whether the domestic courts should follow the domestic law or Community law. The ECJ ruled that the Treaty of Rome required domestic courts to give effect to the directly enforceable provisions of Community law and, in doing so, such courts are required to ignore any national law that runs counter to Community law. The House of Lords then renewed the interim injunction. The ECJ later ruled that in relation to the original referral from the High Court, the Merchant Shipping Act 1988 was contrary to Community law and therefore the Spanish fishing companies should be able to sue for compensation in the UK courts. The subsequent claims also went all the way to the House of Lords before it was finally settled in October 2000 that the UK was liable to pay compensation, which was estimated at between £50 million and £100 million.

SOURCES OF EUROPEAN UNION LAW

Community law, depending on its nature and source, may have direct effect on the domestic laws of its various members; that is, it may be open to individuals to rely on it without the need for their particular state to have enacted the law within its own legal system (see *Factortame*).

There are two types of direct effect. *Vertical direct effect* means that the individual can rely on EU law in any action in relation to their government, but cannot use it against other individuals. *Horizontal direct effect* allows the individual to use the EC provision in an action against other individuals. Other EC provisions only take effect when they have been specifically enacted within the various legal systems within the Community.

The sources of Community law are fourfold:

INTERNAL TREATIES

Internal treaties govern the member states of the EU, and anything contained therein supersedes domestic legal provisions. As was considered previously, the ruling treaties are now:

- *Treaty on European Union* (TEU);
- *Treaty on the Functioning of the European Union* (TFEU);
- *Charter of Fundamental Rights of the European Union* (CFREU).

INTERNATIONAL TREATIES

International treaties are negotiated with other nations by the European Commission on behalf of the EU as a whole and are binding on the individual members of the EU.

SECONDARY LEGISLATION

Secondary legislation is provided for under Art. 249 (formerly 189) of the Treaty of Rome. It provides for three types of legislation to be introduced by the European Council and Commission:

- *Regulations* apply to, and within, member states generally, without the need for those states to pass their own legislation. They are binding and enforceable from the time of their creation and individual states do not have to pass any legislation to give effect to regulations. Thus, in *Macarthys Ltd v Smith* (1979), on a referral from the Court of Appeal to the ECJ, it was held that Art. 157 entitled the plaintiff to assert rights that were not available to her under national legislation, the Equal Pay Act 1970, that had been enacted before the UK had joined the EEC. Whereas the national legislation clearly did not include a comparison between former and present employees, Art. 157's reference to 'equal pay for equal work' did encompass such a situation. Smith was consequently entitled to receive a similar level of remuneration to that of the former male employee who had done her job previously.
- *Directives*, on the other hand, state general goals and leave the precise implementation in the appropriate form to the individual member states. Directives, however, tend to state the means as well as the ends at which they are aimed and the ECJ will give direct effect to directives that are sufficiently clear and complete. See *Van Duyn v Home Office* (1974). Directives usually provide member states with a time limit within which they are required to implement the provision within their own national laws.

If they fail to do so, or implement the directive incompletely, then individuals may be able to cite and rely on the directive in their dealings with the state in question. Further, *Francovich v Italy* (1991) has established that individuals who have suffered as a consequence of a member state's failure to implement Community law may seek damages against that state.

- *Decisions* on the operation of European laws and policies are not intended to have general effect but are aimed at particular states or individuals. They have the force of law under Art. 288.
- Additionally, Art. 17(1) TEU provides scope for the Commission to issue *recommendations* and *opinions* in relation to the operation of Community law. These have no binding force, although they may be taken into account in trying to clarify any ambiguities in domestic law.

JUDGMENTS OF THE EUROPEAN COURT OF JUSTICE

The ECJ is the judicial arm of the EU and, in the field of EU law, its judgments overrule those of national courts. Under Art. 267, national courts have the right to apply to the ECJ for a preliminary ruling on a point of Community law before deciding a case.

The mechanism through which Community law becomes immediately and directly effective in the UK is provided by s. 2(1) of the ECA 1972. Section 2(2) gives power to designated ministers or departments to introduce Orders in Council to give effect to other non-directly-effective Community law.

THE INSTITUTIONS OF THE EUROPEAN UNION

The major institutions of the EU are: the Council of Ministers; the European Parliament; the European Commission; and the ECJ.

THE COUNCIL OF THE EUROPEAN UNION

The Council is made up of ministerial representatives of each of the 27 member states of the EU. The actual composition of the Council varies depending on the nature of the matter to be considered. When considering economic matters, the various states will be represented by their finance ministers or, if the matter before the

Council relates to agriculture, the various agricultural ministers will attend. The organisation of the various specialist councils falls to the President of the Council, currently Herman Von Rompuy. The Foreign Affairs Council, i.e. the meeting of national foreign ministers, is chaired by the Union's High Representative, who is currently Baroness Ashton.

The Council of Ministers is the supreme decision-making body of the EU and, as such, it has the final say in deciding upon EU legislation. Although it acts on recommendations and proposals made to it by the Commission, it does have the power to instruct the Commission to undertake particular investigations and to submit detailed proposals for its consideration.

Council decisions are taken on a mixture of voting procedures. Some measures only require a simple majority; in others, a procedure of qualified majority voting is used; and in yet others, unanimity is required. Qualified majority voting is the procedure in which the votes of the 27 member countries are weighted in proportion to their population from 29 down to 3 votes each: there are a total of 321 votes to be cast.

The SEA (a European treaty legislated into UK law as the European Communities (Amendment) Act 1986) extended the use of qualified majority voting and this was further extended under the Lisbon Treaty, but unanimity is still required in what can be considered as the more politically sensitive areas, such as those relating to the harmonisation of indirect taxation or the free movement of individuals. As the format of particular councils fluctuates, much of its day-to-day work is delegated to a Committee of Permanent Representatives, which operates under the title of COREPER.

THE EUROPEAN PARLIAMENT

The European Parliament is the directly elected European institution and, to that extent, it can be seen as the body that exercises democratic control over the operation of the EU. As in national Parliaments, members are elected to represent constituencies, the elections being held every five years.

The current total number of European Members of Parliament is 785 and the distribution of representation is spread in relation to population. Thus Germany has 99 members of the Parliament, while the UK, France and Italy have 72 each. At the lower end of the representative scale, Luxembourg, Estonia and Cyprus have six representatives each and the smallest member of the Union, Malta, has five members.

The European Parliament's general secretariat is based in Luxembourg, and although the Parliament sits in plenary session in Strasbourg for one week in each month, its detailed and preparatory work is carried out through 18 permanent committees, which usually meet in Brussels. These permanent committees consider proposals from the Commission and provide the full Parliament with reports of such proposals for discussion.

The powers of the European Parliament (the Parliament), however, should not be confused with those of national Parliaments, for the European Parliament is not a legislative institution and, in that respect, it plays a subsidiary role to the Council of Ministers. Originally its powers were merely advisory and supervisory. However, its legislative powers were substantially enhanced by the SEA 1986. Since that enactment, it has had a more influential role to play, particularly in relation to the completion of the internal market. It can now negotiate directly with the Council as to any alterations or amendments it wishes to see in proposed legislation. It can also intervene to question and indeed alter any 'joint position' adopted by the Council on proposals put to it by the Commission. If the Council then insists on pursuing its original 'joint position', it can only do so on the basis of unanimity.

The SEA 1986 also required the assent of Parliament to any international agreements to be entered into by the EU. As a consequence, it has ultimate control not just in relation to trade treaties, but also as regards any future expansion in the EU's membership. The Lisbon Treaty has subsequently further increased the powers of the Parliament, effectively giving it equal power of co-decision with the Council for most legislation, including the budget and agriculture.

The European Parliament is, together with the Council of Ministers, the budgetary authority of the EU. The budget is drawn up by the Commission and is presented to both the Council and the Parliament. As regards what is known as 'obligatory' expenditure, the Council has the final say, but in relation to 'non-obligatory' expenditure, the Parliament has the final decision whether to approve the budget or not. Such budgetary control places the Parliament in an extremely powerful position to influence EU policy, but perhaps the most draconian power the Parliament wields is the ability to pass a vote of censure against the Commission, requiring it to resign en masse.

ECONOMIC AND SOCIAL COMMITTEE

If the Parliament represents the directly elected arm of the EU, then the Economic and Social Committee represents a collection of unelected, but nonetheless influential, interest groups throughout the EU. This Committee is a consultative institution and its opinion must be sought prior to the adoption by the Council of any Commission proposal.

THE EUROPEAN COMMISSION

The European Commission is the executive of the EU and, in that role, it is responsible for the administration of EU policies. There are 27 Commissioners chosen from the various member states to serve for renewable terms of four years. Commissioners are appointed to head departments with specific responsibility for furthering particular areas of EU policy. Once appointed, Commissioners are expected to act in the general interest of the EU as a whole rather than in the partial interest of their own home country.

In pursuit of EU policy, the Commission is responsible for ensuring that Treaty obligations between the member states are met and that Community laws relating to individuals are enforced. In order to fulfil these functions, the Commission has been provided with extensive powers both in relation to the investigation of potential breaches of EU law and the subsequent punishment of offenders. The classic area in which these powers can be seen in operation is competition law. Under Arts 101 and 102 of the TFEU, the Commission has substantial powers to investigate and control potential monopolies and anti-competitive behaviour, and it has used these powers to levy what, in the case of private individuals, would amount to huge fines where breaches of EU competition law have been discovered. As an example, in May 2009 the Commission levied a new record individual fine against the American computer chip manufacturer Intel for abusing its dominance of the microchip market. Intel was accused of using discounts to squeeze its nearest rival, Advanced Micro Devices (AMD), out of the market. The amount of the fine was €1.06bn, equivalent to £950m, or $1.45bn. Intel appealed against the finding and the fine in September 2009.

The Commission also acts, under instructions from the Council, as the negotiator between the EU and external countries.

In addition to these executive functions, the Commission has a vital part to play in the EU's legislative process. The Council can only act on proposals put before it by the Commission. The Commission therefore has a duty to propose to the Council measures that will advance the achievement of the EU's general policies.

THE EUROPEAN COURT OF JUSTICE

The ECJ is the judicial arm of the EU, and in the field of Community law its judgments overrule those of national courts. It consists of 27 judges, one from each member state, assisted by eight Advocates General, and sits in Luxembourg. The role of the Advocate General is to investigate the matter submitted to the Court and to produce a report, together with a recommendation, for the consideration of the Court. The actual Court is free to accept the report or not as it sees fit.

The SEA 1986 provided for a new Court of First Instance to be attached to the existing Court of Justice. Under the Treaty of Lisbon it was renamed the General Court. It has jurisdiction in first instance cases, with appeals going to the ECJ on points of law. The former jurisdiction of the Court of First Instance, in relation to internal claims by EU employees, was transferred to a newly created European Union Civil Service Tribunal in 2004. Together the three distinct courts constitute *the Court of Justice of the European Union*.

The Court of Justice performs two key functions:

(a) It decides whether any measures adopted, or rights denied, by the Commission, Council or any national government are compatible with Treaty obligations. Such actions may be raised by any EU institution, government or individual. In October 2000, the Court of Justice annulled EU Directive 98/43, which required member states to impose a ban on advertising and sponsorship relating to tobacco products, because it had been adopted on the basis of the wrong provisions of the EC Treaty.

A member state may fail to comply with its Treaty obligations in a number of ways. It might fail or indeed refuse to comply with a provision of the Treaty or a regulation; alternatively, it might refuse to implement a directive within the allotted time provided for. Under such circumstances, the state in question will be brought before the ECJ, either by the Commission or another member state or, indeed, individuals within the state concerned.

In 1996, following the outbreak of 'mad cow disease', BSE, in the UK, the European Commission imposed a ban on the export of UK beef. The ban was partially lifted in 1998 and, subject to conditions relating to the documentation of an animal's history prior to slaughter, from 1 August 1999, exports satisfying those conditions were authorised for despatch within the Community. When the French Food Standards Agency continued to raise concerns about the safety of British beef, the Commission issued a protocol agreement, which declared that all meat and meat products from the UK would be distinctively marked as such. However, France continued in its refusal to lift the ban. Subsequently, the Commission applied to the ECJ for a declaration that France was in breach of Community law for failing to lift the prohibition on the sale of correctly labelled British beef in French territory. In December 2001, in *Commission of the European Communities v France*, the ECJ held that the French government had failed to put forward a ground of defence capable of justifying the failure to implement the relevant Decisions and was therefore in breach of Community law.

(b) It provides authoritative rulings, at the request of national courts, under Art. 267 of the TFEU, on the interpretation of points of Community law. When an application is made under Art. 267, the national proceedings are suspended until such time as the determination of the point in question is delivered by the ECJ. While the case is being decided by the ECJ, the national court is expected to provide appropriate interim relief, even if this involves going against a domestic legal provision, as in the *Factortame* case.

The ECJ is not bound by the doctrine of precedent in the same way as UK courts are. It is always open to the ECJ to depart from its previous decisions where it considers it appropriate to do so. Although it will endeavour to maintain consistency, it has, on occasion, ignored its own previous decisions, as in *European Parliament v Council* (1990), where it recognised the right of the Parliament to institute an action against the Council.

THE COURT OF AUDITORS

As its name suggests, it is responsible for providing an external audit of the Community's finances. It examines the legality, regularity and soundness of the management of all the Community's revenue and expenditure.

As we have seen, one relatively small aspect of EU law is to do with human rights. The main source of human rights law in Europe, however, is the European Convention on Human Rights and the European Court of Human Rights – they are not part of the EU machinery. We now turn to examine human rights in the next chapter.

6

HUMAN RIGHTS
THE EUROPEAN CONVENTION AND THE HUMAN RIGHTS ACT 1998

INTRODUCTION

The European Convention on Human Rights and Fundamental Freedoms (hereafter the ECHR) was instituted in 1950. Following the horrific treatment of Jews, among others, by the Nazi regime in Germany the ECHR was introduced as the mechanism for establishing and enforcing essential human rights with the basic hope that they would prevent such horrors in the future. The UK was one of the initial signatories to the ECHR and in 1966, the UK recognised the power of the European Commission on Human Rights to hear complaints from individual UK citizens. At the same time, it recognised the authority of the European Court of Human Rights (ECtHR) to adjudicate in such matters. It did not, however, at that time incorporate the ECHR into UK law.

The consequence of non-incorporation was that the Convention could not be directly enforced in English courts. In *R v Secretary of State for the Home Department ex p Brind* (1991), the Court of Appeal decided that ministerial directives did not have to be construed in line with the ECHR, as that would be tantamount to introducing the ECHR into English law without the necessary legislation. UK citizens were therefore in the position of having to pursue rights that the state endorsed in an external forum rather than through their own court system and, in addition, having to exhaust the domestic judicial procedure before they could gain access to that external forum. Such a situation was extremely unsatisfactory, and not just for complainants under the ECHR. Many members of the judiciary, including the then Lord Chief Justice Lord Bingham, were in favour of incorporation, not merely on general moral grounds, but equally on the ground that they resented having to make decisions in line with UK law which they knew full well would be overturned on appeal to the European Court. Equally, there was some discontent that the decisions in the European Court were being taken, and its general jurisprudence was being developed, without the direct input of the UK legal system. The UK courts, however, were not completely bound to decide cases in presumed ignorance of the ECHR, and did what they could to make decisions in line with it. For example, where domestic statutes were enacted to fulfil ECHR obligations, the courts could, of course, construe the meaning of the statute in the light of the ECHR. It was also possible that, due to the relationship of the ECHR with European Community law, the courts could find themselves applying the former in considering the latter. More indirectly, however, where the common law was uncertain, unclear or incomplete, the courts ruled, wherever possible, in a manner which conformed with the ECHR or, where statute was found to be ambiguous, they presumed that Parliament intended to legislate in conformity with the UK's international obligations under the ECHR. As the late Lord Bingham put it: 'In these ways, the Convention made a clandestine entry into British law by the back door, being forbidden to enter by the front' (Earl Grey Memorial Lecture, http://webjcli.ncl.ac.uk/1998/issue1/bingham1.html).

Even allowing for this degree of judicial manoeuvring, the situation still remained unsatisfactory. Pressure groups did agitate for the incorporation of the ECHR into the UK legal system, but when in 1995 a Private Member's Bill moving for incorporation was introduced in the House of Lords, the Home Office minister, Lady Blatch, expressed the then government's view that such incorporation was 'undesirable and unnecessary, both in principle and practice'. The Labour opposition, however, was committed to the incorporation of the ECHR into UK law and, when it gained office in 1997, it immediately set about the process of incorporation. This process resulted in the Human Rights Act (HRA) 1998.

RIGHTS PROVIDED UNDER THE EUROPEAN CONVENTION ON HUMAN RIGHTS

The Articles incorporated into UK law, and listed in Sched. 1 to the Act, cover the following matters:

THE RIGHT TO LIFE

Article 2 states that 'Everyone's right to life shall be protected by law', consequently there are only very limited circumstances where the state can use force resulting in a person's death. The clearest example of this would be the example of a police officer using no more than reasonable force in self-defence.

PROHIBITION OF TORTURE

Article 3 actually provides that 'No one shall be subjected to torture or to inhuman or degrading treatment or punishment.' This is an absolute prohibition and torture cannot be justified under any circumstances.

PROHIBITION OF SLAVERY AND FORCED LABOUR

Article 4 provides this absolute right.

THE RIGHT TO LIBERTY AND SECURITY

After stating the general right, Article 5 is mainly concerned with the conditions in which individuals can lawfully be deprived of their liberty, the obvious example being where they have been 'fairly tried' and found guilty of a crime.

THE RIGHT TO A FAIR TRIAL

Following on from the previous provision, Article 6 provides that 'everyone is entitled to a fair and public hearing within a reasonable time by an independent and impartial tribunal established by law'. This provision applies equally to both criminal charges and civil cases. Hearings must be heard expeditiously and anyone charged with a criminal offence must be presumed innocent until proven guilty according to law.

THE GENERAL PROHIBITION OF THE ENACTMENT OF RETROSPECTIVE CRIMINAL OFFENCES

Generally, individuals have the right not to be found guilty of a criminal offence arising out of actions which, at the time they were engaged in, were not criminal. Article 7 does, however, recognise the *post hoc* criminalisation of previous behaviour where it is 'criminal according to the general principles of law recognised by civilised nations'.

THE RIGHT TO RESPECT FOR PRIVATE AND FAMILY LIFE

Article 8 expressly extends this right to cover a person's home and correspondence. However, as with many of the provisions of the Convention, there is scope for arguing that it covers, or at least should cover, other areas such as the right to benefit from assisted suicide.

FREEDOM OF THOUGHT, CONSCIENCE AND RELIGION

Article 9 provides individuals with the right to hold views or beliefs, although in limited circumstances the state may limit/control the ways in which such beliefs may be acted on.

FREEDOM OF EXPRESSION

Where Article 9 allows freedom to hold views and opinions, Article 10 protects the right to articulate those views and opinions. The article extends the right to include 'freedom ... to receive and impart information and ideas without interference by public authority and regardless of frontiers', so it applies equally to the listener/recipient as well as the speaker/disseminator of the views and opinions. There are, however, limitations on freedom of expression. While a person is perfectly free to express views that others may find offensive, the state is able to introduce laws that limit the extent of free speech, thus it is a criminal offence to express views that incite racial hatred. Any restriction must be necessary *and* in the pursuit of one of the following:

- the interests of national security,
- public safety,
- the prevention of disorder or crime,
- the protection of health or morals, and
- the protection of the rights and freedoms of others.

The state may also limit Article 11 rights of members of the armed forces, police and civil service to ensure that they retain political neutrality.

FREEDOM OF ASSEMBLY AND ASSOCIATION

Article 11 specifically includes the right to form and join trade unions, but once again, the state is allowed to limit the Article 12 rights of members of the armed forces, police and civil service to ensure that they remain politically neutral.

THE RIGHT TO MARRY

Article 12 establishes the right to marry and to found a family subject to the national laws governing the exercise of this right. Consequently, the state may establish some limits, to the extent of setting marriageable age, and restricting the right to marriage between people of a particular degree of consanguinity.

PROHIBITION OF DISCRIMINATION IN RELATION TO THE ENJOYMENT OF THE RIGHTS AND FREEDOMS SET FORTH IN THE CONVENTION

Article 14 does not provide a distinct substantive right against discrimination, but ensures that public authorities must not apply the substantive rights recognised in the Convention in any way that discriminates against individuals seeking to rely on those rights. The Article specifically refers to discrimination in terms of: 'sex, race, colour, language, religion, political or other opinion, national or social origin, association with a national minority, property, birth'. However, that is not a complete list as it applies equally to any 'other status', which could include, for example, age, disability, sexual orientation.

In addition there are a number of protocols to the Convention which provide the following additional rights:

- the right to peaceful enjoyment of possessions and protection of property (Art. 1 of Protocol 1);
- the right to education (subject to a UK reservation (Art. 2 of Protocol 1));
- the right to free elections (Art. 3 of Protocol 1);
- the right not to be subjected to the death penalty (Arts 1 and 2 of Protocol 6).

The rights listed can be relied on by any person, non-governmental organisation or group of individuals. Importantly, they also apply, where appropriate, to companies that are incorporated entities and hence legal persons. However, they cannot be relied on by governmental organisations, such as local authorities.

THE NATURE OF RIGHTS UNDER THE ACT: DEROGATION, MARGIN OF APPRECIATION AND PROPORTIONALITY

It is apparent that the rights listed above are not all seen in the same way. Some are absolute and inalienable and cannot be interfered with by the state. Others are merely contingent and are subject to *derogation*, that is, signatory states can opt out of them in particular circumstances. The ECtHR also recognises the concept of 'a *margin of appreciation*', which allows for countries to deal with particular problems in the context of their own internal circumstances. The absolute rights are those provided for in Arts 2, 3, 4, 7 and 14. All the others are subject to potential limitations. In particular, the rights provided for under Arts 8, 9, 10 and 11 are subject to legal restrictions such as are 'necessary in a democratic society in the interests of national security or public safety, for the prevention of crime, for the protection of health or morals or the protection of the rights and freedoms of others' (Art. 11(2)).

The UK entered such a derogation in relation to the extended detention of terrorist suspects without charge, under the Prevention of Terrorism (Temporary Provisions) Act 1989, subsequently replaced and extended by the Terrorism Act 2000. Those powers had been held to be contrary to Art. 5 of the Convention by the ECtHR in *Brogan v UK* (1989). The UK also entered a derogation with regard to the Anti-Terrorism, Crime and Security Act 2001, which was enacted in response to the attack on the World Trade Center building in New York on 11 September of that year. The Act allowed for the detention without trial of foreign citizens suspected of being involved in terrorist activity (see further the Belmarsh cases, below).

In deciding the legality of any derogation, courts are required not just to be convinced that there is a need for the derogation, but they must also be sure that the state's action has been *proportionate* to that need. In other words, the state must not overreact to a perceived problem by removing more rights than is necessary to effect the solution. With further regard to the possibility of derogation, s. 19 of the 1998 Act requires a minister, responsible for the passage of any Bill through Parliament, either to make a written declaration that it is compatible with the Convention or, alternatively, to declare that although it may not be compatible, it is still the government's wish to proceed with it.

THE STRUCTURE OF THE HUMAN RIGHTS ACT

The HRA has profound implications for the operation of the English legal system. However, to understand the structure of the HRA, it is essential to be aware of the nature of the changes introduced by the Act, especially in the apparent passing of fundamental powers to the judiciary. Under the doctrine of parliamentary sovereignty, the legislature could pass such laws as it saw fit, even to the extent of removing the rights of its citizens. The 1998 Act reflects a move towards the entrenchment of rights recognised under the Convention, but, given the sensitivity of the relationship between the elected Parliament and the unelected judiciary, it has been thought expedient to minimise the change in the constitutional relationship of Parliament and the judiciary.

Section 2 of the Act requires future courts to take into account any previous decision of the ECtHR. This provision impacts on the operation of the doctrine of precedent within the English legal system, as it effectively sanctions the overruling of any previous English authority that was in conflict with a decision of the ECtHR.

However, in *Price v Leeds City Council* (2006), the House of Lords held that where there were contradictory rulings from it and the European Court of Human Rights, English courts were required to follow the ruling of the House of Lords.

Section 3 requires all legislation to be read, so far as possible, to give effect to the rights provided under the Convention. As will be seen, this section provides the courts with new and extended powers of interpretation. It also has the potential to invalidate previously accepted interpretations of statutes that were made, by necessity, without recourse to the Convention (see *Mendoza v Ghaidan* (2002)).

Section 4 empowers the courts to issue a *declaration of incompatibility* where any piece of primary legislation is found to conflict with the rights provided under the ECHR. This has the effect that the courts cannot invalidate primary legislation, essentially Acts of Parliament but also Orders in Council, which are found to be incompatible; they can only make a declaration of such incompatibility, and leave it to the legislature to remedy the situation through new legislation. Section 10 provides for the provision of remedial legislation through a fast track procedure, which gives a minister of the Crown the power to alter such primary legislation by way of statutory instrument.

Section 5 requires the Crown to be given notice where a court considers issuing a declaration of incompatibility and the appropriate government minister is entitled to be made a party to the case.

Section 6 declares it unlawful for any public authority to act in a way that is incompatible with the ECHR, and consequently the Human Rights Act does not *directly* impose duties on private individuals or companies unless they are performing public functions. Whether or not a private company is performing a public function can prove problematic; there are instances where they would clearly be considered as doing so, such as privatised utility companies providing essential services, or if a private company were to provide prison facilities when it would clearly be operating as a public authority. However, at the other end of an uncertain spectrum, it has been held that, where a local authority fulfils its statutory duty to arrange the provision of care and accommodation for an elderly person through the use of a private care home, the functions performed by the care home are not to be considered as being of a public nature. At least that was the decision of the House of Lords by a majority of three to two in *YL* v *Birmingham City Council* (2007), a surprisingly conservative decision, and one that met with much dismay, given that there was the expectation that the public authority test would be applied generously.

Section 6(3), however, *indirectly* introduces the possibility of horizontal effect into private relationships. As s. 6(3)(a) specifically states that courts and tribunals are public authorities they must therefore act in accordance with the Convention. The consequence of this is that although the HRA does not introduce new causes of action between private individuals the courts, as public authorities, are required to recognise and give effect to their Convention rights in any action that can be raised.

In *R* v *(on the application of Al-Skeini) Secretary of State for Defence* (2007), which related to the conduct of the armed forces in Iraq, the House of Lords held that s. 6 applied to a public body even if it is acting outside the United Kingdom territory, as long as it is acting within the jurisdiction of the United Kingdom, and jurisdiction depends upon control of the relevant location.

Where a public authority is acting under the instructions of some primary legislation, which is itself incompatible with the ECHR, the public authority will not be liable under s. 6.

Section 7 allows the 'victim of the unlawful act' to bring proceedings against the public authority in breach. However, this is interpreted in such a way as to permit relations of the actual victim to initiate proceedings.

Section 8 empowers the court to grant such relief or remedy against the public authority in breach of the Act as it considers just and appropriate. Where a public authority is acting under the instructions of some primary legislation, which is itself incompatible with the ECHR, the public authority will not be liable under s. 6.

Section 10 provides a fast-track means for remedying law that has been found to be incompatible with the provisions, by either a domestic court or the European Court of Human Rights. It gives the appropriate minister the power to alter or remove any such incompatible provision by order, i.e. by delegated legislation.

Section 19 of the Act requires that the minister responsible for the passage of any Bill through Parliament must make a written statement that the provisions of the Bill are compatible with ECHR rights. Alternatively, the minister may make a statement that the Bill does not comply with ECHR rights, but that the government nonetheless intends to proceed with it.

Reactions to the introduction of the HRA have been broadly welcoming, but some important criticisms have been raised. First, the ECHR is a rather old document and does not address some of the issues that contemporary citizens might consider as equally fundamental to those rights actually contained in the document. For example, it is silent on the rights to substantive equality relating to such issues as welfare and access to resources. Also, the actual provisions of the ECHR are uncertain in the extent of their application, or perhaps more crucially in the area where they can be derogated from, and at least to a degree they are contradictory. The most obvious difficulty arises from the need to reconcile Art. 8's right to respect for private and family life with Art. 10's freedom of expression. Newspaper editors have expressed their concern in relation to this particular issue, and fear the development, at the hands of the court, of an overly limiting law of privacy that would prevent investigative journalism. This leads to a further difficulty – the potential politicisation, together with a significant enhancement in power, of the judiciary.

HUMAN RIGHTS CASES

RESTRICTION OF NON-ABSOLUTE RIGHTS AND PROPORTIONALITY

BROWN V STOTT (2001)

In this early case, the claimant had been arrested at a supermarket on suspicion of the theft of a bottle of gin. When the police officers noticed that she smelled of alcohol, they asked her how she had travelled to the store. Brown replied that she had driven and pointed out her car in the supermarket car park. Later, at the police station, the police used their powers under s. 172(2)(a) of the Road Traffic Act 1988 to require her to say who had been driving her car at about 2.30 p.m., that is, at the time when she would have travelled in it to the supermarket. Brown admitted that she had been driving. After a positive breath test, Brown was charged with drink–driving, but appealed to the Scottish High Court of Justiciary for a declaration that the case could not go ahead on the grounds that her admission, as required under s. 172, was contrary to the right to a fair trial under Art. 6 of the ECHR.

In February 2000, the High Court of Justiciary supported her claim on the basis that the right to silence and the right not to incriminate oneself at trial would be worthless if an accused person did not enjoy a right of silence in the course of the criminal investigation leading to the court proceedings. If this were not the case, then the police could require an accused person to provide an incriminating answer which subsequently could be used in evidence against them at their trial. Consequently, the use of evidence obtained under s. 172 of the Road Traffic Act 1988 infringed Brown's rights under Art. 6(1).

Even before the HRA was in operation in England, the Scottish case was followed by a similar ruling in Birmingham Crown Court in July 2000.

The implication of these decisions was extremely serious, not just in relation to drink-driving offences, but also in relation to fines following the capture of speeding cars by traffic cameras. As can be appreciated, the film merely identifies the car; it is s. 172 of the Road Traffic Act that actually requires the compulsory identification of the driver. If *Brown v Stott* stated the law accurately, then the control of speeding cars and drink-driving was in a parlous state.

However, on 5 December 2000, the Privy Council reversed the judgment of the Scottish appeal court in *Brown*. The Privy Council reached its decision on the grounds that the jurisprudence of the ECtHR, established through previous cases, had clearly established that while the overall fairness of a criminal trial could not be compromised, the constituent rights contained in Art. 6 of the ECHR were not themselves absolute and could be restricted in certain limited conditions. Consequently, it was possible for individual states to introduce limited qualification of those rights, so long as they were aimed at 'a clear public objective' and were 'proportionate to the situation' under consideration. The ECHR had to be read as balancing community rights with individual rights. With specific regard to the Road Traffic Act, the objective to be attained was the prevention of injury and death from the misuse of cars, and s. 172 was not a disproportionate response to that objective.

Subsequently, in a majority decision in *O'Halloran v UK* (2007), the European Court of Human Rights approved the use of s. 172 in order to require owners to reveal who had been driving cars caught on speed cameras.

See also the related decision of the House of Lords in *Sheldrake v Director of Public Prosecutions* (2004), which concerned s. 5(2) of the Road Traffic Act 1988 relating to the offence of being in charge of a vehicle after consuming excess alcohol. The court held that s. 5(2) did not require the prosecution to prove that the defendant was likely to drive while intoxicated. Rather the effect of s. 5(2) was to allow the defendant to escape liability if they could prove, on a balance of probabilities, that there was no likelihood of their driving in their intoxicated condition. The House accepted that this interpretation of s. 5(2) infringed the presumption of innocence and introduced a reverse burden of proof, but it considered that such a provision was neither arbitrary nor did it go beyond what was reasonably necessary, given the need to protect the public from the potentially lethal consequences of drink-driving.

JUDICIAL INTERPRETATION OF STATUTES UNDER S. 3 OF THE HRA

RE S *(2002)*

In *Re S*, the Court of Appeal used s. 3 of the HRA in such a way as to create new guidelines for the operation of the Children Act 1989, which increased the courts' powers to intervene in the interests of children taken into care under the Act. This extension of the courts' powers in the pursuit of the improved treatment of such children was achieved by reading the Act in such a way as to allow the courts increased discretion to make interim rather than final care orders, and to establish what were referred to as 'starred milestones' within a child's care plan. If such starred milestones were not achieved within a reasonable time, then the courts could be approached to deliver fresh directions. In effect, what the Court of Appeal was doing was setting up a new, and more active, regime of court supervision in care cases.

The House of Lords, however, although sympathetic to the aims of the Court of Appeal, felt that it had exceeded its powers of interpretation under s. 3 of the HRA and, in its exercise of judicial creativity, it had usurped the function of Parliament.

MENDOZA V GHAIDAN (2002)

In this case the Court of Appeal used s. 3 to extend the rights of same-sex partners to inherit a statutory tenancy under the Rent Act 1977. In *Fitzpatrick v Sterling Housing Association Ltd* (1999), the House of Lords had extended the rights of such individuals to inherit the lesser assured tenancy by including them within the deceased person's family. It declined to allow them to inherit statutory tenancies, however, on the grounds that they could not be considered to be the wife or husband of the deceased as the Act required. In *Mendoza*, the Court of Appeal held that the Rent Act, as it had been construed by the House of Lords in *Fitzpatrick*, was incompatible with Art. 14 of the ECHR on the grounds of its discriminatory treatment of surviving same-sex partners. The court, however, decided that the failing could be remedied by reading the words 'as his or her wife or husband' in the Act as meaning 'as if they were his or her wife or husband'. *Mendoza* is of particular interest in the fact that it shows how the HRA can permit lower courts to avoid previous and otherwise binding decisions of the House of Lords. It also clearly shows the extent to which s. 3 increases the powers of the judiciary in relation to statutory interpretation.

In spite of this potential increased power, the House of Lords found itself unable to use s. 3 in *Bellinger v Bellinger* (2003). The case related to the rights of transsexuals and the court found itself unable, or at least unwilling, to interpret s. 11(c) of the Matrimonial Causes Act 1973 in such a way as to allow a male-to-female transsexual to be treated in law as a female. Nonetheless, the court did issue a declaration of incompatibility.

DECLARATIONS OF INCOMPATIBILITY UNDER S. 4 OF THE HRA

As has been stated previously, the courts are not able to declare primary legislation invalid, but, as an alternative, they may make a declaration that the legislation in question is not compatible with the rights provided by the ECHR.

R V (1) MENTAL HEALTH REVIEW TRIBUNAL, NORTH & EAST LONDON REGION (2) SECRETARY OF STATE FOR HEALTH EX P H

The first declaration of incompatibility was issued in this case in March 2001, in which the Court of Appeal held that ss 72 and 73 of the Mental Health Act 1983 were incompatible with Art. 5(1) and (4) of the ECHR in as much as they reversed the normal burden of proof, by requiring the detained person to show that they should not be detained rather than the authorities to show that they should be detained.

A V SECRETARY OF STATE FOR THE HOME DEPARTMENT (HOUSE OF LORDS) *(2004)*

Following the terrorist attack on the World Trade Center on 11 September 2001, the UK Parliament introduced the Anti-Terrorism, Crime and Security Act (ACSA) 2001. This Act allowed for the detention, without charge, of non-UK citizens suspected of terrorist activities, but who could not be repatriated to their own countries because of fear for their well-being.

While a person who would otherwise be detained was free to leave the United Kingdom, the Act provided that a person certificated as a suspected international terrorist under s. 21 might be detained in circumstances where their safe removal or departure from the UK was not practical (s. 23(1)).

Such a provision was clearly contrary to Art. 5 of the ECHR. Consequently, the government was required to enter a derogation from the Convention by virtue of the Human Rights Act 1998 (Designated Derogation) Order 2001, the justification for the derogation being that the prospect of terrorism following 11 September 2001 threatened the life of the nation.

When consideration of the powers of detention under ACSA ultimately came before the House of Lords it resulted in a crushing judgment against the Act and an undisguised and unmitigated rebuke to the government and its anti-terrorism policies. The strength of the decision was almost startling, especially in the light of the previously more accommodating decisions of the Court of Appeal in relation to state policy. The case was heard by a panel of nine Law Lords, Lord Steyn having stood down from the appeal because he had previously expressed the view that the derogation was unjustified, and it decided by a majority of 8:1, only Lord Walker dissenting, that the ACSA was incompatible with the provisions of the ECHR.

Although the House of Lords recognised the deference due to the government and parliament and accepted that the government had been entitled to conclude that there was a public emergency, it nonetheless concluded that the response to the perceived threat had been disproportionate and incompatible with the rights under the ECHR.

It held that the prohibition on grounds of nationality or immigration status, under Art. 14, had not been the subject of derogation. Further, it held that the decision to detain one group of suspected international terrorists, defined by nationality or immigration status, and not another could not be justified, and violated Art. 14 of the ECHR. In relation to the discriminatory effect of the Act, the House pointed out the illogicality at its heart for, if the potential threat to the security of the UK *by UK nationals* suspected of being Al Qa'ida terrorists could be addressed without infringing their right to personal liberty, then why could not similar measures be used to deal with any threat presented by *foreign nationals*?

The House of Lords also held that ss 21 and 23 of the Act were *disproportionate* for the general reason that the provisions did not rationally address the threat to the security of the UK presented by Al Qa'ida terrorists. This general conclusion was supported by a number of particular shortcomings within the Act, such as the facts that:

- it did not address the threat presented by UK nationals;
- it permitted foreign nationals suspected of being Al Qa'ida terrorists to pursue their activities abroad if there was any country to which they were able to go.

As a result of this reasoning, the House of Lords decided that s. 23 of the ACSA was incompatible with Art. 5 and Art. 14 of the ECHR and appropriately quashed the Derogation Order 2001, as it was secondary rather than primary legislation.

Human rights, then, is a theme which crops up all over English law. Its principles should be something every citizen should understand. One of the most democratic aspects of the justice system is the institution of the jury and it is that topic which we turn to in the next chapter.

7

THE JURY

INTRODUCTION

It is generally accepted that the jury of '12 good men and true' lies at the heart of the British legal system. The implicit assumption is that the presence of 12 ordinary laypersons, randomly introduced into the trial procedure to be the arbiters of the facts of the case, strengthens the legitimacy of the legal system. It supposedly achieves this end by introducing a democratic, humanising element into the abstract, impersonal trial process, thereby reducing the exclusive power of the legal professionals who would otherwise command the legal stage and control the legal procedure without reference to the opinion of the lay majority.

Having defended the institution of the jury generally, it has to be recognised that there are particular instances that tend to bring the jury system into disrepute. For example, in October 1994, the Court of Appeal ordered the retrial of a man convicted of double murder on the grounds that four of the jurors had attempted to contact the alleged victims using a Ouija board in what was described as a 'drunken experiment' (*R v Young* (1995)). A second convicted murderer appealed against his conviction on the grounds of irregularities in the manner in which the jury performed its functions. Among the allegations levelled at the jury was the claim that they clubbed together and spent £150 on drink when they were sent to a hotel after failing to reach a verdict. It was alleged that some of the jurors discussed the case against the express instructions of the judge and that on the following day, the jury foreman had to be replaced because she was too hung-over to act. One female juror was alleged to have ended up in bed with another hotel guest.

A truly remarkable case came to light in December 2000 when a trial that had been going on for 10 weeks was stopped on the grounds that a female juror was conducting what were referred to as 'improper relations' with a male member of the jury protection force who had been allocated to look after the jury during the trial. The relationship had become apparent after the other members of the jury had found out that they were using their mobile phones to send text messages to one another during breaks in the trial. That aborted trial was estimated to have cost £1.5 million, but it emerged that this was the second time the case had to be stopped on account of inappropriate behaviour on the part of jury members. The first trial had been abandoned after some of the jury were found playing cards when they should have been deliberating on the case.

Another example of the possible criticisms to be levelled against the misuse of juries occurred in Stoke-on-Trent, where the son of a court usher and another six individuals were found to have served on a number of criminal trial juries. While one could praise the public-spirited nature of this dedication to the justice process, especially given the difficulty in getting members of jury panels, it might be more appropriate to condemn the possibility of the emergence of a professional juror system connected to court officials. Certainly, the Court of Appeal was less than happy with the situation, and overturned a conviction when the Stoke practice was revealed to it.

THE ROLE OF THE JURY

It is generally accepted that the function of the jury is to decide on matters of fact, and that matters of law are the province of the judge. Such may be the ideal case, but most of the time, the jury's decision is based on a consideration of a mixture of fact and law.

The jurors determine whether a person is guilty on the basis of their understanding of the law as explained to them by the judge.

The oath taken by each juror states that they 'will faithfully try the defendant and give a true verdict according to the evidence', and it is contempt of court for a juror subsequent to being sworn in to refuse to come to a decision.

Judges have the power to direct juries to acquit the accused where there is insufficient evidence to convict them, and this is the main safeguard against juries finding defendants guilty in spite of either the absence, or the insufficiency, of the evidence. There is, however, no corresponding judicial power to instruct juries to convict (*DPP v Stonehouse* (1978); *R v Wang* (2005)). That being said, there is nothing to prevent the judge summing up in such a way as to make it evident to the jury that there is only one decision that can reasonably be made, and that it would be perverse to reach any other verdict but guilty.

What judges must not do is overtly put pressure on juries to reach guilty verdicts. Finding of any such pressure will result in the overturning of any conviction so obtained. The classic example of such a case is *R v McKenna* (1960), in which the judge told the jurors, after they had spent all of two and a quarter hours deliberating on the issue, that if they did not come up with a verdict in the following 10 minutes, they would be locked up for the night. Not surprisingly, the jury returned a verdict; unfortunately for the defendant, it was a guilty verdict; even more unfortunately for the judicial process, the conviction had to be quashed on appeal for clear interference with the jury.

JURORS' EQUITY?

In criminal cases, even perversity of decision does not provide grounds for appeal against acquittal. There have been occasions where juries have been subjected to the invective of a judge when they have delivered a verdict with which he disagreed. Nonetheless, the fact is that juries collectively, and individual jurors, do not have to justify, explain or even give reasons for their decisions. Indeed, under s. 8 of the Contempt of Court Act 1981, it would be a contempt of court to try to elicit such information from a jury member in either a criminal or a civil law case.

These factors place juries in a very strong position to take decisions that are 'unjustifiable' in accordance with the law, for the simple reason that they do not have to justify the decisions. In September 2008 six Greenpeace climate change activists were cleared of causing £30,000 of criminal damage at a coal-fired power station in Kent. They had admitted trying to shut down the station by occupying the smokestack and painting the word 'Gordon' down the chimney. However, the jury found them not guilty on the basis of their defence, which was that they were justified in their action as they were acting to prevent climate change causing greater damage to property around the world. In his summing-up at the end of an eight-day trial, the judge, David Caddick, said the case centred on whether or not the protesters had a lawful excuse for their actions and the jury found that they did.

A non-political example of this type of case can be seen in the jury's refusal to find Stephen Owen guilty of any offence after he had discharged a shotgun at the driver of a lorry that had killed his child. And, in September 2000, a jury in Carlisle found Lesley Gibson not guilty on a charge of possession of cannabis after she told the court that she needed it to relieve the symptoms of the multiple sclerosis from which she suffered. The tendency of the jury occasionally to ignore legal formality in favour of substantive justice is one of the major points in favour of its retention, according to its proponents.

APPEALS FROM DECISIONS OF THE JURY

In criminal law, it is an absolute rule that there can be no appeal against a jury's decision to acquit a person of the charges laid against him. Although there is no appeal as such against acquittal, there does exist the possibility of the Attorney-General referring the case to the Court of Appeal, to seek its advice on points of law raised in criminal cases in which the defendant has been acquitted. This procedure was provided for under s. 36 of the CJA 1972, although it is not commonly resorted to. It must be stressed that there is no possibility of the actual case being reheard or the acquittal decision being reversed, but the procedure can highlight mistakes in law made in the course of Crown Court trial and permits the Court of Appeal to remedy the defect for the future.

In civil law cases, the possibility of the jury's verdict being over-turned on appeal does exist, but only in circumstances where the original verdict was perverse, that is, no reasonable jury properly directed could have made such a decision.

MAJORITY VERDICTS

The possibility of a jury deciding a case on the basis of a majority decision was introduced by the CJA 1967. Prior to this, the requirement was that jury decisions had to be unanimous. Such decisions are acceptable where there are:

- not less than 11 jurors and 10 of them agree; or
- there are 10 jurors and nine of them agree.

Where a jury has reached a guilty verdict on the basis of a majority decision, s. 17(3) of the Juries Act (JA) 1974 requires the foreman of the jury to state in open court the number of jurors who agreed and the number who disagreed with the verdict (*R v Barry* (1975)).

DISCHARGE OF JURORS OR THE JURY

The trial judge may discharge the whole jury if certain irregularities occur. These would include the situation where the defendant's previous convictions are revealed inadvertently during the trial. Such a disclosure would be prejudicial to the defendant. In such a case, the trial would be ordered to commence again with a different jury. Individual jurors may be discharged by the judge if they are incapable of continuing to act through illness 'or for any other reason' (s. 16(1) of the Juries Act (JA) 1974). Where this happens, the jury must not fall below nine members.

THE SELECTION OF THE JURY

In theory, jury service is a public duty that citizens should rea-dily undertake. In practice, it is made compulsory, and failure to perform one's civic responsibility is subject to the sanction of a £1,000 fine.

LIABILITY TO SERVE

Any person between the ages of 18 and 70, who is on the electoral register and who has lived in the UK for at least five years, is qualified to serve as a juror.

The procedure for establishing a jury is a threefold process:

- An officer of the court summons a *randomly* selected number of qualified individuals from the electoral register.
- From that group, panels of potential jurors for various cases are drawn up.
- The actual jurors are then *randomly* selected by means of a ballot in open court.

As regards the actual random nature of the selection process, a number of problems arise from the use of electoral registers to determine and locate jurors:

- Electoral registers tend to be inaccurate. Generally, they misreport the number of younger people who are in an area simply because younger people tend to move about more than older people.
- Electoral registers tend to underreport the number of members of ethnic minorities in a community.

INELIGIBILITY EXCEPTIONS, DISQUALIFICATION AND EXCUSAL

Prior to the CJA 2003, the general qualification for serving as a juror was subject to a number of exceptions.

INELIGIBILITY

A variety of people were deemed to be ineligible to serve on juries on the basis of their employment or vocation. Among this category were: judges; Justices of the Peace; members of the legal profession; police and probation officers; and members of the clergy or religious orders. Those suffering from a mental disorder were also deemed to be ineligible. Paragraph 2 of Sched. 33 to the CJA 2003 removes the first three groups of persons ineligible, the judiciary, others concerned with the administration of justice, and the clergy, leaving only mentally disordered persons with that status.

DISQUALIFICATION

In an endeavour to maintain the unquestioned probity of the jury system, certain categories of persons are disqualified from serving as jurors. Among these are anyone who has been sentenced to a term of imprisonment, or youth custody, of five years or more. In addition, those on bail in criminal proceedings are disqualified from serving as a juror in the Crown Court.

EXCUSAL

Following the CJA 2003, no one is entitled to excusal as of right from jury service. However, it remains the case that if a person who has been summoned to do jury service can show 'good reason' they may be deferred or excused.

CHALLENGES TO JURY MEMBERSHIP

Both prosecution and defence have a right to challenge the array where the summoning officer has acted improperly in bringing the whole panel together. Such challenges are rare (see *R v Danvers* (1982)).

CHALLENGE BY THE DEFENCE

Until the CJA 1988, there were two ways in which the defence could challenge potential jurors:

PEREMPTORY CHALLENGE

The defence could object to any potential jury members, up to a maximum number of three, without having to show any reason or justification for the challenge.

CHALLENGE FOR CAUSE

The defence retains the power to challenge any number of potential jurors for cause, that is to say that there is a substantial reason why a particular person should not serve on the jury to decide a particular defendant's case.

CHALLENGE BY THE PROSECUTION

While the prosecution has the same right as the defence to challenge for cause, it has the additional option of excluding potential jury members by simply asking them to stand by until a jury has been empanelled. The request for the potential juror to stand by is only a provisional challenge and, in theory, the person stood by can at a later time take their place on the jury if there are no other suitable candidates. In practice, of course, it is unlikely in the extreme for there not to be sufficient alternative candidates to whom the prosecution do not object and prefer to the person stood by.

JURY VETTING

Jury vetting is the process by which the Crown checks the background of potential jurors to assess their suitability to decide particular cases. The procedure is clearly contrary to the ideal of the jury being based on a random selection of people, but it is justified on the basis that it is necessary to ensure that jury members are not likely to divulge any secrets made open to them in the course of a sensitive trial or, alternatively, on the ground that jurors with extreme political views should not be permitted the opportunity to express those views in a situation where they might influence the outcome of a case.

THE RACIAL MIX OF THE JURY

In *R v Danvers* (1982), the defence had sought to challenge the array on the basis that a black defendant could not have complete confidence in the impartiality of an all-white jury. The question of the racial mix of a jury has exercised the courts on a number of occasions. In *R v Ford* (1989), the trial judge's refusal to accept the defendant's application for a racially mixed jury was supported by the Court of Appeal on the grounds that 'fairness is achieved by the principle of random selection' as regards the make-up of a jury, and that to insist on a racially balanced jury would be contrary to that principle, and would be to imply that particular jurors were incapable of impartiality. A similar point was made in *R v Tarrant* (1997), in which a person accused of drug-related offences was convicted by a jury that had been selected from outside the normal catchment area for the court. The aim of the judge had been to minimise potential jury intimidation, but nonetheless, the Court of Appeal overturned the conviction on the grounds that the judge had deprived the defendant of a randomly selected jury.

In February 2010 the report on empirical research carried out by Professor Cheryl Thomas for the Ministry of Justice suggested that:

> While these findings strongly suggest that racially balanced juries are *not needed* to ensure fair decision-making in jury trials with BME (black and minority ethnic) defendants, concerns about *the appearance of fairness* with all-White juries may still remain.
>
> (emphasis added)

THE DECLINE OF THE JURY TRIAL

Many direct attempts have been made in the recent past to reduce the operation of the jury system within the English legal system. These particular endeavours, however, have to be understood in the context of the general historical decline in the use of the jury as the mechanism for determining issues in court cases.

THE JURY TRIAL IN CIVIL PROCEDURE

In respect of civil law, the use of juries has diminished considerably and automatic recourse to trial by jury is restricted to a small number of areas and, even in those areas, the continued use of the jury is threatened. At present the right to a jury trial is limited to only four specific areas:

- fraud,
- defamation,
- malicious prosecution, and
- false imprisonment.

Even in these areas, the right is not absolute and can be denied where the case involves 'any prolonged examination of documents or accounts or any scientific or local investigation which cannot conveniently be made with a jury'.

The right to jury trial in defamation cases has been the object of particular criticism, and in 1996 statute law intervened in the form of the Defamation Act, which was designed to simplify the procedure of defamation cases and gave new powers for judges to deal with cases without a jury.

JURIES IN CRIMINAL TRIALS

It has to be borne in mind that the criminal jury trial is essentially the creature of the crown court, and that the magistrates' courts deal with at least 95 per cent of criminal cases. In practice, juries determine the outcome of less than 1 per cent of the total of criminal cases. It can be seen, therefore, that in absolute and proportional terms, the jury does not play a significant part in the determination of criminal cases. If trial by jury is not statistically significant, it cannot be denied that it is of major significance in the determination of the most serious cases. Even this role, however, has not gone without scrutiny, as will be seen below.

CRIMINAL JUSTICE ACT 2003: JURY TAMPERING

The term 'jury tampering' covers a range of circumstances in which the jury's independence is or may appear to be compromised. Such a situation could come about because of actual harm or threats of harm to jury members. It might equally involve intimidation or bribery of jury members. Alternatively, it could also include similar improper approaches to a juror's family or friends. Sections 44 and 46 of the CJA 2003 provide for a trial on indictment in the crown court to be conducted without a jury where there is a danger of jury tampering, or continued without a jury where the jury has been discharged because of jury tampering. A trial without a jury was used in the case of Peter Blake and others accused of a major robbery and where jury interference was suspected (*The Times*, 19th February 2010).

CRIMINAL JUSTICE ACT 2003: COMPLEX FRAUD TRIALS

The Roskill Committee on Fraud Trials (1986) recommended the abolition of trial by jury in complex fraud cases and this possibility has been on the political agenda ever since. However, the CJA 2003 introduced measures much more restrictive than any previous body had recommended, s. 43 allowing the prosecution to apply for a serious or complex fraud trial on indictment in the crown court to proceed in the absence of a jury. This provision has not as yet come into effect as it requires a positive vote in favour, by both the House of Commons and the House of Lords.

INVESTIGATION OF JURY BEHAVIOUR

The very first recommendation made by the Runciman Commission on Criminal Justice was that s. 8 of the Contempt of Court Act 1981 should be repealed to enable research to be conducted into juries' reasons for their verdicts. Section 8 makes it an offence to obtain, disclose or solicit any particulars of statements made, opinion expressed, arguments advanced or votes cast by members of a jury in the course of their deliberations in any legal proceedings.

In *Attorney-General v Associated Newspapers* (1994), the House of Lords held that it was contempt of court for a newspaper to publish disclosures by jurors of what took place in the jury room while they were considering their verdict, unless the publication amounted to no more than a restatement of facts already known. It was decided that the word 'disclose' in s. 8(1) applied not just to jurors, but to any others who published their revelations.

The continued legality of s. 8 in the light of Art. 6 of the ECHR was considered in *R v Mirza* in January 2004. The appellant Mirza had been convicted on six counts of indecent assault by a majority verdict of 10:2. He had arrived in the UK from Pakistan in 1988 and, during the trial, he had made use of an interpreter. During the course of the trial, the jury sent a note asking the interpreter whether it was typical of a man with Mirza's background to require an interpreter, despite having lived in the UK for so long. It was explained to the jury that it was usual for people who were not fluent to have an interpreter in complicated and serious cases and, in his summing up, the judge directed the jury not to draw an adverse inference from Mirza's use of an interpreter.

Six days after the case finished, the defence counsel received a letter from one of the jurors claiming that some jurors had, from the beginning of the trial, believed that the use of the interpreter had been a devious ploy. The question of the interpreter was raised early during the jury's deliberations, and the letter writer was 'shouted down' when she objected and sought to remind the other members of the jury of the judge's directions. Members of the jury specifically refused to accept the judge's direction, and some regarded defence counsel's warnings against prejudice in her final speech as 'playing the race card'. The writer concluded that the decision of the jury was that of bigots who considered Mirza guilty because he used an interpreter in court after declining one for his police interviews.

When the case came on appeal to the House of Lords, it was confirmed by a majority of 4:1 that s. 8 of the Contempt of Court Act 1981 prevented any investigation into what had taken place within the confines of the jury room.

THE USE OF THE INTERNET AND OTHER ELECTRONIC MEANS OF COMMUNICATIONS

There has always been a possibility of jurors being influenced by extraneous sources of information, such as press or other media sources, rather than solely relying on the evidence presented in the court. However, the growth of information technology has intensified the problem and generated particular difficulties in relation to juries. In *R v Adem Karakaya* (2005) the Court of Appeal held that material downloaded from the internet and taken into a jury room by one of the members of a jury was contrary to the general rule that jurors were not to rely on privately obtained information or to receive further information after it had retired.

Subsequently in *R v Thakrar* (2008) a member of a jury supplied fellow jury members with information, again found on the internet, about the defendant's previous convictions. Unfortunately the information was incorrect. Just over six weeks into the trial, and at the conclusion of the appellant's examination-in-chief, the jury passed a note to the judge, which revealed that they had received the information from the internet. The judge directed the jury in strong terms that they must disregard the internet information and they went on to find the accused guilty. However, on appeal it was held that there should be a retrial as in the circumstances there was a real possibility that a member, or members, of the jury did not follow the direction given by the judge.

The subject of jurors using the internet and mobile communications to research cases and in particular details relating to the accused in cases became a major issue in the course of 2010. In her report on the fairness of juries, released in February 2010, Cheryl Thomas found that in high-profile cases almost three-quarters of jurors will be aware of media coverage of their case. However, the report raised questions about the issue of internet use by jury members in particular. The research revealed that:

- all jurors who looked for information about their case during the trial looked on the internet;
- more jurors said they saw information on the internet than admitted looking for it on the internet;
- in high-profile cases 26 per cent said they saw information on the internet compared to 12 per cent who said they looked, whereas in standard cases 13 per cent said they saw information compared to 5 per cent who said they looked.

As Thomas pointed out, as jurors were admitting to doing something they should have been told by the judge not to do, that may explain why more jurors said they 'just saw' reports on the internet than said they 'looked' on the internet.

Interesting and important as these findings were, they did not generate the same degree of heat that subsequent interventions did.

In October 2010, a former Director of Public Prosecutions, now Lord Ken McDonald, engaged in a public debate on the matter by expressing the view that:

This is a serious point and we struggled with it, in criminal justice, for years trying to protect juries from what they might read about a case on the internet, material they weren't supposed to know about while they were trying it ... In essence, we're finally giving up and just concluding that you have to expect juries to try cases fairly and they're told to do that so I think this is a serious issue around privacy, because policing the internet is really, I think, an unmanageable task. I don't think juries should be 'allowed' to do online research, but I do think we need to assume this will occasionally happen and that it should not invalidate a trial. We have to expect them to follow directions to try the case on the evidence. Otherwise, jury trial will go.

Lord McDonald's comments prompted the Lord Chief Justice to intervene with his own views in a lecture delivered to the Judicial Studies Board of Northern Ireland on 16 November 2010, entitled simply 'Jury Trials' available at http://www.judiciary.gov.uk/NR/

rdonlyres/CBB8FE3E-ACEB-49EE-B004-A0AAD2AAC3F8/0/
speechlcjjurytrialsjsblecturebelfast.pdf.

In his speech Judge LCJ makes his view clear (the use of LCJ after a judge's name means he or she is the Lord Chief Justice. In this case the judge's surname happens to be Judge):

> What we seem to do at the moment, is to assume that the occasions when jurors go to the internet for information are rare indeed. It is therefore easy to brush them aside as odd moments of aberration. I wonder whether we will still be thinking that in a year or two from now. Professor Thomas suggests that we should be thinking of it immediately. I respectfully agree.
>
> I should just add that I must record my entire disagreement with the view of the former Director of Public Prosecutions in England and Wales, now Lord McDonald, that judges are 'giving up trying to stop jurors using Google, Facebook and Twitter to access potentially false and prejudicial' information about defendants. He is reported as suggesting that a trial should not be invalidated if jurors are found to have conducted online research while a case is in progress.

Not only does Lord Judge appear to agree with Professor Thomas that there is a problem but he also appears to agree with her proposed solution. As she suggested in her report:

> To address both jury impropriety in general and juror use of the internet, the judiciary and HMCS should consider issuing every sworn juror with written guidelines clearly outlining the requirements for serving on a trial.

In the words of Judge LCJ:

> I have to be blunt about this, but in my view, if the jury system is to survive as the system for a fair trial in which we all believe and support, the misuse of the internet by jurors must stop. And I think we must spell this out to them yet more clearly. It must be provided in the information received by every potential juror. It must be reflected in the video which jurors see before they start a trial. Judges must continue to direct juries in unequivocal terms from the very outset of

the trial. And I should like the notice in jury rooms which identifies potential contempt of court arising from discussions outside the jury room of their debates, to be extended to any form of reference to the internet.

CONCLUSION

It has been repeatedly suggested by those in favour of abolishing, or at least severely curtailing, the role of the jury in the criminal justice system, that the general perception of the jury is romanticised and has little foundation in reality. Runciman did not actually make this point explicitly, but it is implicit in his assessment of the jury system as against the magistrates' courts. Others have been more explicit; thus, the Roskill Committee expressed the view that 'Society appears to have an attachment to jury trial which is emotional or sentimental rather than logical' (para 8.21).

A similar point had been made previously by the Faulks Committee, but that report also recognised the source of the public's opinion and was careful not to dismiss it as unimportant: 'Much of the support for jury trials is emotional and derives from the undoubted value of juries in serious criminal cases where they stand between the prosecuting authority and the citizen' (para 496).

The jury system certainly commands considerable public support. A survey published in January 2004, involving interviews with 361 jurors, found that, for the vast majority of respondents, juries were seen as an essential component of providing a fair and just trial process, and the diversity of the jury was seen as the best way of avoiding bias and arriving at a sound verdict. The major conclusions of the survey were as follows:

- The majority of respondents had a more positive view of the jury trial system after completing their service than they did before. Furthermore, despite the considerable personal inconvenience they may have suffered, virtually all jurors interviewed considered jury trials to be an important part of the criminal justice system.
- Confidence in the jury system was closely associated with the process, fairness, respect for the rights of defendants and ability of all the members of the jury to consider evidence from

different perspectives. A jury's representation of a broad spectrum of views was a key factor in jurors' confidence in the crown court trial.

- Jurors were very impressed with the professionalism and help-fulness of the court personnel. In particular, they praised the judge's performance, commitment and competence.
- The main impediment to understanding proceedings was the use of legal terminology, although jurors also felt that evidence could sometimes be presented more clearly.
- Over half of the respondents said that they would be happy to do jury service again, while 19 per cent said that they 'would not mind' doing it again. The most positive aspects of engaging in jury service were reported to be having a greater under-standing of the criminal court trial, a feeling of having performed an important civic duty and finding the experience personally fulfilling.

The ideological power of the jury system should not be under-estimated. It represents the ordinary person's input into the legal system and it is at least arguable that in that way, it provides the whole legal system with a sense of legitimacy. It is argued by some civil libertarians that the existence of the non-jury Diplock courts in Northern Ireland brings the whole of the legal system in that province into disrepute. Diplock courts were technically abolished in 2007 but non-jury trials can be used if jurors are believed to be at risk of intimidation. Between 1 August 2008 and 31 July 2009, 13 non-jury trials were held, down from 29 in the previous year.

As Lord Devlin noted (*Trial By Jury*, 1966):

> The first object of any tyrant in Whitehall would be to make Parliament utterly subservient to his will; and the next to overthrow or diminish trial by jury, for no tyrant could afford to leave a subject's freedom in the hands of 12 of his countrymen.

Having examined the workings of the jury we now move on to the next chapter in which we examine the criminal law – something which juries spend much of their time aiming to understand.

8

CRIMINAL LAW

WHAT IS CRIMINAL LAW?

Criminal law prohibits crime, but what is a crime? In one way, it is impossible to formulate a universal definition of crime because the essence of criminality changes over history.

Lending money and charging interest used to be the crime of usury. Perpetrators were punished. Nowadays bankers and financiers successful in lending money might attract peerages not punishment. Cocaine was once a legal narcotic used both for recreational purposes and toothache; now it is illegal. As one writer (Glanville Williams) put it: 'a crime (or offence) is a legal wrong that can be followed by criminal proceedings which may result in punishment'. In other words, a crime is anything that the state has chosen to criminalise. A similar analysis was adopted by the judge Lord Atkin. He said that the scope of the criminal law can only be ascertained by looking at

what acts at any particular period are declared by the State to be crimes, and the only common nature they will be found to possess is that they are prohibited by the State and that those who commit them are punished.

One way to escape going round in circles with these definitions of crime is to refer to the seriousness of the wrongs. So, Glanville

Williams eventually concedes that 'a crime is an act that is condemned sufficiently strongly to have induced the authorities (legislature or judges) to declare it to be punishable before the ordinary courts'.

All sorts of social, religious, moral and technological factors affect which behaviours are criminalised. Today, offences include activities that for various reasons were not crimes in earlier ages such as selling glue to children, computer offences and insider trading.

There are about 11,000 criminal offences in English law. They range from the most minor traffic offences (for example, driving a vehicle with one of the rear brake lights not working) to genocide (criminalised under the Genocide Act 1969). These different criminal offences have no common denominator other than that they are things the state has, for different reasons and at different times, decided are sufficiently serious to warrant being treated as crimes.

Much of the criminal law is now to be found in Acts of Parliament (often called statutes), though there are a number of offences such as murder and manslaughter, and defences such as automatism, intoxication and duress, which depend largely upon decisions of the courts and have not been formulated in legislation. There is certainly no all-embracing code of criminal law, even though proposals for putting all the law in one code (codification) were made as long ago as the nineteenth century. The Law Commission, a governmental law reform body, has revived attempts to devise a Code and has been publishing proposals since 1989, but they have not yet been enacted.

WHO GETS PROSECUTED?

Not every criminal act results in someone being prosecuted. The authorities have a professional discretion whether to proceed. Every day, thousands of people are on tenterhooks awaiting a life-changing decision on whether a prosecution will be brought.

In February, 2007, along with others, Warner Segura, a 20-year-old criminal gang member in the Costa Rican city of Limón, jumped a group of elderly American tourists and tried to rob them. He viciously threatened them with a gun and a knife. The victims were terrified. One of the group, a 70-year-old man who was a martial arts fighter and ex-marine, grabbed Segura in a headlock, and killed him with his bare hands by snapping his neck. Francisco Ruiz, a spokesman for Costa Rica's Judicial Investigation Police, said: 'No charges will be pressed in this case, it is a case of self-defence in which the lives of many tourists may have been saved.'

You can argue about whether it was necessary as an act of self-defence to kill Segura but it seems extremely unlikely that if the hero had been tried for homicide he would have been convicted.

In English law, the police have a very significant discretion as to what to do when a crime has apparently been committed. They can turn a blind eye, caution the suspect, or charge him. In 1951, the Attorney-General, Lord Shawcross, noted that: 'It has never been the rule in this country – I hope it never will be – that suspected criminal offences must automatically be the subject of prosecution.'

The exercising of the prosecutor's discretion can be contentious. In 1995, for example, Gary Lewis, an impoverished father, was prosecuted at a cost of £750, after he stole six lumps of coal to keep warm his newborn baby. In 2007, Judge John Dowse halted a trial, which had cost taxpayers £60,000, indicating it should never have been brought. A chip shop owner, who thought he was doing his public duty, had carried out a citizen's arrest on a 12-year-old delinquent who spat at customers and smashed a window. He was prosecuted for kidnapping the boy (for six minutes) while waiting for the police. The judge said it had not been in the public interest for the prosecution to have been brought. Exercised badly, the discretion to prosecute brings the law into contempt.

The Crown Prosecution Service decides whether to prosecute any case file it gets from the police according to principles set out in the Code for Crown Prosecutors. This requires two tests to be satisfied.

First, there must be a 'realistic prospect of conviction' (the evidential test). Prosecutors must predict what a magistrates' bench, or a jury properly directed by the judge, would be likely to decide. If a conviction is predicted as 'more likely than not', then the case can proceed. In making the decision, prosecutors must assess whether the evidence on file would be admissible in court (so it cannot, for example, be hearsay), and, if it is admissible, whether it is reliable evidence. This evidential test to decide whether to bring a case is different from that used by a court if and when the case *is* prosecuted.

If the case gets to court, there can only be a conviction if the magistrates or jury are 'sure' of the defendant's guilt.

Second, if there *is* enough evidence to provide a realistic prospect of conviction, then a 'public interest' test must also be satisfied. The Code states that in cases of any seriousness, a prosecution will usually take place 'unless there are public interest factors tending against prosecution which clearly outweigh those tending in favour'. Prosecutors must balance factors for and against prosecution carefully and fairly.

The Code lists 17 common 'public interest factors in favour of prosecution'. They include cases where:

- the offence was committed against a person serving the public, like a police officer or a nurse;
- the offence, although not serious in itself, is widespread in the area where it was committed;
- there is evidence that the offence was carried out by a group.

The Code also lists nine factors bearing against a prosecution. These include circumstances where:

- the court is likely to impose a very small or nominal penalty;
- the offence was committed as a result of a genuine mistake or misunderstanding (judged against the seriousness of the offence);
- the loss or harm can be described as minor and was the result of a single incident, particularly if it was caused by a misjudgement.

Deciding on the public interest is, the Code says, 'not simply a matter of adding up the number of factors on each side'. This is like much else in the law, which commonly requires the *evaluation* rather than the simple counting of factors on either side of an argument. As Chief Justice Kenyon noted in 1800, 'It is a canticle of courts of justice that witnesses *non numerentur sed ponderentur*, they are not to be numbered but weighed.'

CLASSIFICATION OF CRIMES

There are a number of ways of classifying crimes. The more common ways of doing so include the following:

- by source – conduct criminalised by judge-made 'common law' contrasted with statutory offences which have been criminalised by Parliament;
- by method of trial – summary (tried by magistrates), indictable (triable before a jury) and triable 'either way' depending on how serious a version of the crime something is (e.g. was it theft of a tyre or theft of a fleet of supermarket lorries?);
- by reference to the powers of arrest – whether they are 'arrestable' or 'non-arrestable', essentially whether the police have the power to arrest for the offence without a warrant;
- by whether they can be regarded as 'true' crimes or merely as 'regulatory' crimes – this classification can be valuable in considering whether a crime should be seen as imposing 'strict liability' which means liability that doesn't depend on the perpetrator's frame of mind. Offences of strict liability include speeding and selling alcohol to minors.

THE ELEMENTS OF CRIMINAL LIABILITY

Criminal liability consists of three main components:

- criminal behaviour accompanied by
- a guilty mind and
- the absence of a defence.

The Latin principle *actus non facit reum nisi mens sit rea* means 'an act does not make a person guilty unless his mind is guilty'. Mental awareness or an intent amounting to a guilty mind is a necessary ingredient for almost all crimes. For the purposes of working out whether defendants are guilty of crimes, the meaning of this Latin phrase is broken down into two components: the *actus reus* is the conduct part of the crime and the *mens rea* is the mental element.

1. The *actus reus* – some 'conduct' by D (for 'defendant', the person who ends up getting charged) accompanied by the existence of legally relevant 'circumstances'. For many offences, it will also be necessary to show that the conduct 'caused' certain 'consequences'. These are the external elements of an offence

and, in the traditional terminology, they comprise the *actus reus* of the offence. For example, D elbows V (for victim) in the face. V is a police constable on duty. This is the *actus reus* of assaulting a police constable in the execution of his duty. The conduct is the elbowing, the consequence is that force is inflicted on V and the circumstances are that V was not just any person (which would have made it a common assault) but a police constable acting in the execution of his duty.

2. The *mens rea* – a blameworthy state of mind in relation to the conduct, circumstances and consequences (that is, to the *actus reus* elements identified above). Traditionally, this blameworthy state of mind is referred to as *mens rea* and includes such varieties as intention and recklessness (awareness of risk) and, in very limited cases, recklessness without awareness of risk. In the example above, if D was trying to elbow V in the face, he intended to inflict force. If he knew there was a risk that he would elbow V in the face (if, for instance, he had his back to V and swung his elbow back in V's direction to keep him away), he was reckless as to the infliction of force.

3. The absence of any defence, whether general or specific, total or partial, which D could plead to avoid liability. In the example previously discussed, suppose that V was not wearing a uniform and that D thought V was an ordinary member of the public who was about to attack him. He would be entitled to use reasonable force to defend himself. So, D might avoid liability for elbowing V in the face (the issues of mistake and self-defence are discussed later in this chapter).

THE *ACTUS REUS*

The *actus reus* of a crime is not merely any *act* by D. Criminal liability does not always require proof of an act. In some situations, an *omission to act* will be enough. This is why the broader term 'conduct' is used in discussing *actus reus*. For example, D can kill by an act such as beating, shooting or stabbing, but he may do so by withholding food from someone who is helpless. This is an omission.

It is also usual to qualify 'conduct' by asserting that it must be 'voluntary', that is, it is at least in part the product of control by the conscious brain. So, 'voluntariness' is another element in the *actus reus* of crimes. If D is feeling a little unwell and clumsily breaks a vase on sale in a shop, he is probably still acting voluntarily because he has some conscious control of his movements. If, instead, he had received a severe blow to the head moments before he broke the vase, it may be that he was not acting voluntarily because he was concussed.

The *actus reus* includes any elements appearing in the definition of the crime which are neither conduct nor consequences. These elements are generally called 'circumstances'. As explained above, in the offence of assaulting a police constable in the execution of his duty, V must have two special characteristics: he must be a police officer and he must be performing his duty. These are 'circumstances' to be proved, as required by the definition of the crime.

The *actus reus* of many crimes will incorporate a required 'consequence' which must be 'caused' by D's conduct. If D kicks out at V, he will only commit the *actus reus* of inflicting grievous bodily harm if the kick lands on V and causes him serious injury. D may miss with his kick, or he may kick V and cause him only minor injury. In either case, there will be no offence of inflicting grievous bodily harm (though there may be an offence of attempt).

A general way of expressing all of this might be to say that the *actus reus* of a crime consists of all those elements which cannot be described as part of the *mens rea*.

CAN AN OMISSION TO ACT AMOUNT TO CRIMINAL CONDUCT?

Criminal liability generally depends upon proof that someone engaged in some act. If we think about crimes such as murder, causing grievous bodily harm with intent and theft, we imagine acts such as shooting, stabbing, kicking or punching V, or stealthily removing V's wallet from his pocket or taking items from a shop. Most of us grow up accepting the idea that we are forbidden from doing some things, however much we might want to do them. We absorb notions of prohibition and punishment from an early age and so we're familiar with the general structure of criminal law and criminal justice. So, criminal liability based on the prohibition of *acts* creates no special problems.

By contrast, we find it difficult to imagine the factual situations in which crimes may be committed by *failures* to act (that is, omissions). How is it possible to say, for instance, that D killed V by not doing something? If D fails to help V who has been knocked down by a hit-and-run driver and is bleeding to death, how does that failure *cause* V's death? To believe that D could be responsible, we have to persuade ourselves that he ought to have intervened. But, however much we might feel morally obliged to help others, we are not accustomed to thinking that there is a general legal obligation to do so. In any case, what exactly would D be required to do, and would the same obligation be placed on every other bystander who was aware of V's injuries? Would all of them be prosecuted if they failed to help? If so, then the criminal justice system might be overwhelmed. If not, selective prosecution might bring the system into disrepute.

On the other hand, there are some situations in which we have no difficulty in regarding others as responsible for harmful consequences when they *fail* to act. A parent, for example, is expected to be vigilant for the health and safety of their child. In 2008, at Welshpool magistrates' court in Wales, a woman was convicted of wilfully neglecting her child. She had abandoned her 14-year-old daughter while she slid off to Greece for a six-week jaunt with a young boyfriend. The mother left her child in a house with no hot water, £100 and some frozen meals. The mother knew the child was in a sexual relationship but was evidently unconcerned.

How caring does the law specify that a parent must be? Sensibly, it doesn't supply a complete code of care but simply forbids things like 'wilful neglect'. The word 'wilful' here means the parent was aware that their neglect would put their child's health at risk. It also covers the indifferent parent who is not aware that their neglect will risk their child's health only because they don't care at all about such risks.

Prosecutions can be brought under the Children and Young Persons Act 1933 if someone who is 16 or over (usually an adult parent) wilfully neglects anyone under 16 for whom they are responsible. The crime occurs if the parent wilfully assaults, ill-treats, neglects or abandons the child in a way 'likely to cause him unnecessary suffering or injury to health'. The phrase 'injury to health' includes physical injury or suffering or 'mental derangement'. The offence carries a sentence of up to 10 years' imprisonment.

This legislation relies on case law to define its key words. The word 'abandon' in the Act means 'to leave a child to its fate'. In a case in 1957, Edward Boulden was convicted of abandoning and neglecting his five children (aged between one and nine) in their home in Feltham, outside London. After an argument, his wife left their home to go to Glasgow. Later, Mr Boulden left the home and phoned the National Society for the Prevention of Cruelty to Children (NSPCC) to say his children were alone. He'd left them all in the unlit house with little food (two loaves, two pints of milk, one egg), and gone to Glasgow after his wife. He was sentenced to six months' imprisonment.

A parent can be convicted even when a child suffering, or the likelihood of it suffering, was avoided by the arrival of another person (as in the Boulden case where the police arrived the day the father left), or where the victim actually died.

Under the law, a parent is deemed to have neglected a child 'in manner likely to cause injury to his health' if he has failed to provide adequate food, clothing, medical aid or lodging. And it's not necessarily a defence for an accused parent to say suffering wouldn't have happened if an agency had stepped in to help. In a case in 1896, a man earning £1 a week spent it all on drink, except about 3s (15p) a week, which he gave to his wife for her and the support of their four children. The wife was unable to supply the children with enough food and clothing and they suffered in health as a result. The court rejected an argument from the father that harm wouldn't have occurred if the mother had sought help under the poor law.

The law does not fix any specific age below 16 at which children can be left at home alone. It needs to be flexible because, while some 12-year-old people can be very mature, some 15-year-olds are very immature. Home-alone cases are judged on all their particular facts.

Apart from parents being obliged to act to help their children, people in other roles sometimes have an obligation to act to protect people. A swimming pool supervisor, for example, is expected to act to ensure the safety of swimmers.

The difference between the witness to the hit-and-run incident (above) and the parent or swimming pool supervisor is easy to see. Nothing marks out the witness to the accident from any other witness. Why should he or she be given an obligation to act? The law would have to adopt a very wide idea of what people are obliged to do to help others in order to impose liability on him (though some countries do recognise obligations of this kind). To impose liability on the parent or supervisor, however, is to recognise an obligation grounded in a pre-existing relationship between parent and child, or supervisor and swimmer, into which parent and supervisor have entered (more or less) freely. It does not imply that anyone else is under the obligation.

GENERAL DEFENCES

A general defence is one which may be raised to all, or at least to most, crimes, unlike a defence such as diminished responsibility, which relates only to the offence of murder. Where a general defence is successfully pleaded, the usual effect is that D avoids liability entirely. The basis of the defences varies. For instance, automatism is a denial that the prosecution has established one of the main elements of the *actus reus* (that D's conduct must be voluntary). Intoxication, on the other hand, is usually introduced to deny that the prosecution has established the *mens rea*. Insanity may operate as a denial of either or both (though recent cases suggest that it only operates to deny *mens rea*, and so cannot be used where the offence is one of strict liability), or simply as a claim to be excused from liability because of a failure to perceive that the conduct was 'wrong'. In pleading self-defence, however, D admits the *actus reus* and the *mens rea* but claims to be justified in what he did.

Some commentators see such a justificatory defence as denying that the conduct was in any way 'unlawful' (some crimes expressly incorporate the word 'unlawful' in their definition, though it might be argued that all crimes implicitly incorporate the requirement). Similarly, in duress or duress of circumstances (where someone says they were forced to commit a crime by someone else or by circumstances), D admits *actus reus* and *mens rea* but claims to be justified, or at any rate excused, because of the pressure applied to him by others or by the circumstances.

The burden of proof in these defences is generally on the prosecution; that is, once the defence has been introduced, the prosecution must disprove it. Even so, D usually has to present some credible evidence in support of the defence before the prosecution is put to the task of disproving it. The defence of insanity is an exception to this rule about burden of proof. The burden is on D to prove that he was insane at the time of the commission of the alleged offence. The following discussion is confined to a consideration of issues relating to intoxication, given the close association between intoxication and certain offences.

INTOXICATION

A plea of intoxication presents particular difficulties for the criminal law. On the one hand, it is generally acknowledged that a great deal of criminal behaviour, especially behaviour consisting of spontaneous acts of personal violence, aggression and damage to property, is associated with consumption of alcohol and drugs. There is also evidence to suggest that intoxication may be a factor in many instances of theft, robbery and burglary, which may be motivated by a need for funds to sustain drug-taking habits. Why allow D to plead intoxication when intoxication may be the very root of the problem? On the other hand, the Crown must prove all the elements of an offence. If D is intoxicated, so that one of those elements might not be present (intention or recklessness, say), why should D be prevented from introducing evidence of the intoxication?

A first step in confronting this dilemma is to make two crucial distinctions:

- between substances which are regarded as intoxicants and substances which are not; and
- between intoxication for which D is responsible (is at fault) (voluntary intoxication) and intoxication for which he is not (involuntary intoxication).

SUBSTANCES WHICH ARE INTOXICANTS

Put in simple terms, any substance which is commonly known to produce the kind of effects generally associated with intoxication can be regarded as an intoxicant. These effects include changes of mood, perception and consciousness, reduction in inhibitions, impaired ability for self-control, reduction in motor skills and ability to react, and increased difficulty in forming judgements and assessing the consequences of actions. They are characteristic of the consumption of alcohol and drugs (both medical and recreational), and also of other substances such as glues and solvents.

A substance may be regarded as an intoxicant when it produces the effects which would be expected of it, but not when it produces entirely unexpected effects.

In *R v Hardie* (1985) the Court of Appeal considered the case of Paul Hardie, who had been convicted of criminal damage. He had taken a number of Valium tablets (which were prescribed for someone else) and started a fire in the flat he shared with his partner – but from whom he was separating. The court allowed his appeal and quashed his conviction. It ruled that what he did in taking the pills did not necessarily amount to voluntary intoxication. It ruled:

> [Valium is] wholly different in kind from drugs which are liable to cause unpredictability or aggressiveness ... if the effect of a drug is merely soporific or sedative the taking of it, even in some excessive quantity, cannot in the ordinary way raise a conclusive presumption against the admission of proof of intoxication for the purpose of disproving *mens rea*. ... [The jury] should have been directed that if they came to the conclusion that, as a result of the Valium, the appellant was, at the time, unable to appreciate the risks to property and persons from his actions they should then consider whether the taking of the Valium was itself reckless.

So, the tranquilliser was not an intoxicant in relation to the wholly unexpected violent and aggressive behaviour, but would have been had the issue been about impaired perception and responses caused by the expected tranquillising effects.

Where D suffers intoxication effects from consumption of a substance which is not an intoxicant, he may introduce the explanation in evidence as he would introduce any other explanation to cast doubt on the Crown's case.

VOLUNTARY AND INVOLUNTARY INTOXICATION

D will be voluntarily intoxicated where he was consuming a substance which he knew or should have known (it is commonly known) to be an intoxicant. He will be held to be voluntarily intoxicated even if he makes a mistake about the strength of the intoxicant. In *Allen*

(1988), D's claim to have underestimated the alcoholic content of the wine he was drinking, and so not to have been voluntarily intoxicated, was rejected. It was enough that he knew that he was drinking wine. If D consumes a medical drug that can be characterised as an intoxicant and either does not follow medical advice or the drug has not been prescribed for him, then this will probably be voluntary intoxication.

Conversely, D will be involuntarily intoxicated when he has consumed an intoxicant without knowing that he has consumed the substance at all or, perhaps, when he neither knew nor should have known that it was an intoxicant. The obvious examples are where D's non-alcoholic drink is 'spiked' without his knowledge with alcohol or some drug, and where he innocently eats food to which a drug has been added. A further example ought to be where, without D's knowledge, a different intoxicant is added to the intoxicating substance he knows himself to be consuming, as where a mildly alcoholic drink is spiked with stronger alcohol or a drug. Theoretically, this is significantly different from the situation in *Allen*, discussed above, though the practical distinction might be hard to make.

LIABILITY WHERE D IS INVOLUNTARILY INTOXICATED

In cases of involuntary intoxication, the rule is that D is entitled to introduce evidence of the intoxication to refute the Crown's allegation of *mens rea*, whether the offence requires proof of intention or recklessness. But the effect of the intoxication must be that D did not form the required *mens rea*. D cannot claim that, though he knew what he was doing, he would not have done it but for the intoxication. Even though D could claim that it was not his fault in such a case, the broader excuse thus created would be difficult to fit within the existing legal framework and would generate considerable problems of proof. The rules on involuntary intoxication were established by the House of Lords in *Kingston* (1994) when restoring D's conviction for indecently assaulting a youth after it had been quashed by the Court of Appeal. D had claimed that he had been drugged without his knowledge as part of a deliberate plot to exploit his suppressed homosexual paedophilic tendencies and had only given way to them because of the drug. The House of Lords held that the Crown was only required to prove *mens rea* in the conventional sense and did not have to prove some extra element of moral fault.

LIABILITY WHERE D IS VOLUNTARILY INTOXICATED

The current rules on the effect of voluntary intoxication were established by the House of Lords in *DPP v Majewski* (1976). In this leading judgment, the House of Lords decided that a person who commits a crime but doesn't know what he's doing because he is so inebriated can still be convicted if it is not necessary to prove intention for that particular crime. During the course of a disturbance at a pub in Basildon, Essex, Robert Majewski attacked the landlord and two other people, injuring all three of them. When the police arrived, he assaulted an officer, and later, at the police station where he had been taken, he struck two other officers. He was charged with various assaults. At his trial he testified that during the 48 hours preceding the disturbance he had taken a considerable quantity of drugs and that, at the time when the assaults were committed, he was acting under a combination of amphetamines, barbiturates and alcohol. He didn't know what he was doing and had no recollection of the incidents in question. He was convicted and his appeal was dismissed. The Lords held that unless the offence was one that required proof of a specific intent, it was no defence that the accused didn't intend to commit the act alleged. His recklessness was enough to convict him.

The rules provide that offences are divided into two categories, *specific intent* on the one hand, *basic intent* on the other. Specific intent offences are satisfied by proof of nothing less than an intention. They include murder, causing grievous bodily harm with intent to cause such harm, theft and robbery. Basic intent offences are satisfied by proof of recklessness and include manslaughter, inflicting grievous bodily harm, assault occasioning actual bodily harm, assault, battery and criminal damage. Some offences are specific intent offences as to one element but basic intent as to another. Thus, rape requires proof of intention to have sexual intercourse but merely recklessness as to V's lack of consent; if D is charged with a specific intent offence, he may introduce evidence of intoxication in asserting that, at the time of the offence, he did not have the required intention.

This does not mean that anyone who was drunk inevitably avoids liability for such an offence. The effect of the intoxication must be evaluated by the jury and D avoids liability if it tends to show that he did not form the intention. As is well known, intoxication often simply makes people more aggressive or less inhibited and, if this was the case, it would not assist D. On the other hand, the issue is whether D did or did not form the intention; it is not whether he was capable of forming any intention at all. This distinction is important because D may argue that he did not form the *particular* intention, whilst being prepared to concede that he had formed *some* intention. In *Brown and Stratton* (1998), the trial judge erred in directing the jury that a plea of intoxication would only be relevant if D was saying, 'I was so drunk on this occasion that I was almost unconscious and I was not capable of forming any intention at all.' D's conviction for causing grievous bodily harm with intent was quashed and a conviction for the lesser offence of inflicting grievous bodily harm (requiring proof only of intention or recklessness as to some harm and, as such, a basic intent offence) was substituted.

If D is charged with a basic intent offence, he is not allowed simply to introduce evidence of intoxication to explain why he was not aware of a risk (was not reckless). Consequently, if he has no other independent argument to advance, it is almost certain that he will be convicted. The Court of Appeal has stated that the Crown must prove that D would have foreseen the risk had he not been intoxicated (*Richardson and Irwin* (1999)). A person who raises evidence of intoxication to avoid conviction for a specific intent offence will inevitably be convicted of any associated basic intent offence.

The House of Lords in *Majewski* sought to justify this approach to the effect of voluntary intoxication on criminal liability by suggesting that voluntary consumption of intoxicants is itself a reckless course of conduct which supplies the *mens rea* element that was apparently lacking at the time of commission of the offence. Clearly, this rather general recklessness has little in common with the awareness of particular risks usually necessary in proof of *mens rea*. It might be more realistic to accept that a policy decision has been made in which the courts have tried to strike a balance between practical and theoretical concerns. The balance depends upon the arbitrary division of offences into specific and basic intent, to which distinct rules of liability are then applied when intoxication is in issue.

MISTAKE

For the most part, D's plea of mistake is merely a denial of *mens rea*. In saying that he made a mistake, D means that he could not have intended or known of the risk of a consequence, or known, or have been aware of the risk of the existence of a particular circumstance. If the offence requires proof of intention/knowledge or subjective recklessness, then an honest mistake is evidence of lack of *mens rea*. If the offence is satisfied by proof of objective recklessness or negligence, then only an honest and reasonable mistake will suffice. This approach to mistake was confirmed by the House of Lords in *DPP v Morgan* (1975), where it was held that D could not be guilty of rape if he genuinely, albeit mistakenly, believed that V was consenting. His belief did not have to be reasonable, though, of course, a reasonable mistake is more likely to be perceived as a genuine mistake.

Despite the controversy generated by the ruling, D's conviction for rape was actually upheld because his belief that V was consenting was not credible. His argument had been that he genuinely believed her to be consenting, despite obvious evidence to the contrary, because V's husband had invited him to have sexual intercourse with V and had told him to expect some resistance because 'that was how [V] liked it'.

An alternative way in which mistake may be of relevance is where D pleads a defence which he cannot sustain on the actual facts but argues that it would have been available had the facts been as D mistakenly believed them to be (this is the same kind of situation as that discussed above). The courts have not applied a uniform rule to this kind of claim. In self-defence, for instance, D is entitled to be judged on the facts as he genuinely believed them to be. In *Beckford* (1987), D, a police officer, shot and killed a suspect, V, in the mistaken belief that V was armed and was about to shoot at D. The issue was not whether D's belief was reasonable but simply whether it was genuine. If so, was his response a use of proportionate force in the circumstances that he believed existed? By contrast, the courts have demanded that mistakes made in the context of the defence of duress must be reasonable. So, if D mistakenly believes that there is a threat of death or serious injury to himself or another, his defence will fail if the mistake is unreasonable (*Graham* (1982)).

In a case in 1994, the Court of Appeal held that a rape conviction should stand where a woman had sex with a man whom she mistakenly thought was her boyfriend. Ziani Elbekkay, the culprit, was sentenced to five years' imprisonment. The victim, a 30-year-old woman, had lived in Hackney in London with her boyfriend for 18 months. Elbekkay was staying the night with them. All three had been drinking. The boyfriend fell asleep in another room. During the night, the woman said she was awakened by someone moving on the bed and touching her. She assumed it was her boyfriend and, without opening her eyes, said 'I love you'. Intercourse then began and after about 20 seconds they kissed. Thinking something was not quite right, she opened her eyes and saw that it wasn't her boyfriend. She punched Elbekkay and cut him with a knife.

In that case, the woman wasn't too drunk to know what was happening. If, though, a complainant was too drunk to remember whether she (or he, as male rape is the same crime) consented then the prosecution will fall. In 2005, a rape case at Swansea crown court collapsed after a 21-year-old student told the court that she had been too drunk to remember whether or not she had agreed to have sex with the defendant. She had alleged she was raped by a fellow student in a corridor of a hall of residence at Aberystwyth University.

The defendant, who said that the corridor sex was consensual, had been escorting her to her room from a party after she became very drunk. In court she said if she'd wanted sex she would have opened her flat door and taken the man into her bedroom. But she admitted passing out after drinking too much. Mr Justice Roderick Evans directed the jury to reach a not guilty verdict, on the basis that drunken consent is still consent.

What about where a man makes a drunken mistake that the person he has sex with is consenting? The legal answer, quite reasonably, is that such an excuse usually won't wash. The underlying reasoning is this: a man can be convicted of rape not only when he has sex knowing the other person isn't consenting but also where he has been criminally reckless about whether there is consent or not.

Therefore, if a man gets so drunk he can't tell whether someone is consenting he won't have an excuse because bingeing itself is reckless.

Technically, though, a defendant can only be convicted of rape if he did not 'reasonably believe' that the other person consented. That's to stop sly people who have forced themselves on someone being able to get away with it by saying 'personally, I did happen to believe she was consenting' even where such a belief was madly unreasonable. But as being drunk doesn't necessarily stop someone having a 'reasonable belief' (although it usually does), it is just possible for a jury to acquit a man whose slightly drunken belief in consent was nevertheless, in the view of the jury, reasonable. Unlikely, but possible.

SELF-DEFENCE/PREVENTION OF CRIME

The rule that a person may use reasonable force to defend himself and his property is long established and is firmly rooted in our beliefs about our rights. Its application to particular facts, however, can often prove very difficult. In recent years, much controversy has been provoked by the criminal prosecution of ordinary people who allegedly used excessive force, usually involving a weapon, to protect themselves or their property from determined criminals.

In December 2009, Munir Hussain was sentenced to 30 months' imprisonment for violently attacking Walid Salem, a thug who broke into his home, tied up his family, and threatened to kill them during a robbery.

In January 2010, the Court of Appeal freed Mr Hussain noting that the case was one of 'true exceptionality'. In 'an act of mercy' and acknowledging the intense public 'call for mercy' the Court commuted Mr Hussain's 30-month sentence to one year and suspended it for two years. The Lord Chief Justice noted that while the principle 'that you cannot take the law into your own hands without punishment' must be upheld, this was a case in which it was proper for the Court's judgment to 'reflect the principles of justice and mercy'. Mr Hussain's brother, Tokeer, had also been convicted of serious assault for the attack on the burglar and he was sentenced to 39 months' imprisonment. On appeal his sentence was reduced to two years but not suspended; it was relevant to recognise that the brother had not himself been the victim of any crime.

Many people will say the thug whom the brothers attacked got what he deserved and the law was an ass to prosecute the Hussain brothers. The visceral outrage which many people would experience if their home was broken into and the lives of their loved ones put under threat is undeniable. The law, though, is not soft: it *does* allow people to use violence to repel criminals. Even extreme violence is legally permitted in some circumstances; if you're facing a night-time intruder in your bedroom and he's holding a knife, the law doesn't demand you try to disarm him using only a moral dialogue.

What the law does not permit is chasing after a criminal after he has fled the crime scene, bringing him to the ground and then, with several accomplices, beating him with a cricket bat and metal rod until he has a broken skull and brain damage. That is what Hussain, his brother and other accomplices did to the thug Salem. That isn't self-defence; that is vigilante punishment. Some people might still ask 'but why is that wrong – surely if a criminal breaks into your home he becomes fair game?' The answer is that if the law permitted that approach we would rapidly descend into violent chaos and mayhem. The law would have to stand back and watch as life was punctuated by punishment beatings and community vigilantism.

Section 76 of the Criminal Justice and Immigration Act 2008 allows anyone accused of a violent crime a defence if he honestly believed it was necessary to use force and if the degree of force used was not disproportionate in the circumstances as he viewed them. A person who uses force is judged on the basis of the circumstances as he perceived them. In the heat of the moment he will not be expected to have judged exactly what action was called for, and a degree of latitude may be given to someone who only did what he honestly and instinctively thought was necessary. If he hit an intruder with a hockey stick, the law won't deny him a defence on the basis that he could have repelled the intruder with a mere cricket stump.

In 1604, in a case about what force could be used to defend a home, a judge said: 'The house of everyone is to him as his castle and fortress' (Semayne's case, 5 Co. Rep. at 91b). The decision established the principle that an Englishman's home is his castle. That is still true but private punishment is not allowed. In 1604, more violent 'self-defence' was permitted because there was no police force or system of public prosecutions. The first Director of Public Prosecutions was appointed in 1880. The society of 1604, though, should no more be a model for today's law than it should be a model for today's dentistry or employment practices.

Guidance issued in 2005 by the Crown Prosecution Service and the Association of Chief Police Officers says that anyone can use reasonable force to protect themselves or others or to prevent crime. It is based on the common law and section 3 of the Criminal Law Act 1967. A citizen isn't expected to make fine judgements over the level of force used in the heat of the moment. The official advice says:

> So long as you only do what you honestly and instinctively believe is necessary in the heat of the moment, that would be the strongest evidence of you acting lawfully and in self-defence. This is still the case if you use something to hand as a weapon.

Someone at home and under threat does not have to wait to be attacked. He can strike first. But he should not be too pre-emptive. In 1988, Ted Newberry, a 76-year-old from Ilkeston, Derbyshire, lay in wait in his allotment shed for an expected intruder, then shot a 12-bore gun at a Mark Revill when he tried to enter. Revill was badly injured and Mr Newberry was prosecuted on charges of wounding, but was acquitted by a jury. The injured intruder, however, won compensation for his injuries (the award was £12,000 reduced to £4,000 because of his contributory negligence) even though he had been acting criminally. The pre-emptive action was not excused by the civil law.

Current CPS guidelines for prosecutors are helpfully clear and sensible (http://www.cps.gov.uk/legal/s_to_u/self_defence/#Use_of_Force_1). They say, under 'Use of Force against Those Committing Crime', that in deciding whether to prosecute, prosecutors should have particular regard to:

> the nature of the offence being committed by the victim; *the degree of excessiveness of the force used by the accused*; the extent of the injuries, and the loss or damage, sustained by either or both parties to the incident; *whether the accused was making an honest albeit over zealous attempt to*

*uphold the law rather than taking the law into his own hands for the purposes
of revenge or retribution.*

(emphasis added)

The play of these principles in court has produced various results –
sometimes resulting in *convictions* and sometimes *exoneration* for
self-defenders. Although expressed in 2005 and 2009 the principles
in issue have been extant for decades.

Tony Martin, a Norfolk farmer, was convicted of murder in
1999 for shooting a young burglar in the back. On appeal, Martin's
conviction was reduced to manslaughter (on the grounds of
diminished responsibility) and he was released in 2003. In another
case in 2000, David Summers was caught by the men into whose
Peterborough flat he had broken. In their fearful defence they
inflicted multiple injuries on him with a metal baseball bat.
Sentencing Summers to a year in jail for burglary, Judge Hugh
Mayor, QC, said he would not reduce Summers' sentence on
account of the injuries he had suffered. He said: 'They used reasonable
force ... You brought that on yourself and I have no sympathy for
those who receive hurt while committing a crime.' That sort of
approach has a long history. For example, between 1300 and 1348
homicide was the third most common offence prosecuted in
England but there were frequent acquittals where householders had
killed housebreakers.

In 2005, the Director of Public Prosecutions stated that during
the previous 15 years (when the courts dealt with over 20 million
crimes) there had only been 11 prosecutions against householders
for excessive violence in response to a crime including one in
which a burglar was tied up, thrown in a pit and set alight.

The rule on force in the prevention of crime is expressed in s. 3 of
the Criminal Law Act 1967:

A person may use such force as is reasonable in the circumstances
in the prevention of crime, or in effecting or assisting in the lawful
arrest of offenders or suspected offenders or of persons unlawfully
at large.

The courts have gradually modified the common law defence of
self-defence to bring its rules into line with the statutory requirement

for prevention of crime. In doing so, they have removed special rules dealing, for instance, with the duty to 'retreat' before striking a blow in self-defence.

There is no restriction to the offences to which self-defence/prevention of crime can be a defence. In particular, the defence can be, and often is, pleaded to a charge of murder. However, if D kills when using more force than is proportionate, even though some force was necessary, he will lose the defence entirely and will be convicted of murder, not merely of manslaughter. This proposition was starkly illustrated in the case of *Clegg* (1995), where a British soldier serving in Northern Ireland shot at a car which had broken through a checkpoint, killing a passenger. It subsequently emerged that the driver and passengers were joyriders, not terrorists. D was adjudged to have used excessive force, since the danger to other soldiers from the speeding car or anything its occupants might do had passed once the car had cleared the checkpoint. Accordingly, D's conviction for murder was upheld (later developments saw D's conviction quashed and his acquittal at a re-trial but his conviction for lesser offences arising out of the incident).

The old rules on self-defence required D to retreat if at all possible, at any rate before using deadly force. Evidence that D did retreat or did try to avoid a physical confrontation is certainly powerful evidence that he was not the aggressor and that what he did truly was done in self-defence. Even so, the modern rule is merely that it must be necessary to use force. If retreat or negotiation were possible, then force may not have been necessary. But retreat or attempts to talk may only delay the inevitable and, sometimes, striking the first blow may be the most effective form of defence. Indeed, in some cases, not to strike the first blow may be to invite inevitable disaster. These realities were recognised in *Bird* (1985), where the Court of Appeal held that there is no duty to seek to avoid a confrontation (whether by retreat or other means). The court therefore considered that even if D had struck the first blow in lashing out at V with a glass whilst being restrained by him, that was not inconsistent with the notion of self-defence.

Equally, D will not lose the defence simply because he knowingly 'walked into trouble'. A person is not required to avoid going to places where he may lawfully go but where he knows that danger may await, as occurred in *Field* (1972). In that case, D went to a café despite having been warned that V and others were waiting for him there. Nor is evidence that D was unlawfully in possession of a weapon necessarily fatal to the defence. It would be absurd to suggest that force was necessary in self-defence but that, in using proportionate force, D should not be able to use whatever was to hand. In both cases, of course, such evidence may reduce the credibility of D's claim to have been acting in self-defence or in the prevention of crime.

We have looked in this chapter at criminal law – the law under which the state prosecutes alleged criminals with a view to getting them convicted and punished. In the next chapter we turn to look at a very different type of law – the law of contract, which governs the agreements citizens and organisations make with one another.

9

CONTRACT LAW

INTRODUCTION

Ours is a market system. This means that economic activity takes place through the exchange of commodities. Individual possessors of commodities meet in the marketplace and freely enter into negotiations to determine the terms on which they are willing to exchange those commodities. Contract law may be seen as the mechanism for facilitating, regulating and enforcing such market activities.

It is usual for textbooks to cite how all our daily transactions, from buying a newspaper or riding on a bus to our employment, are all examples of contracts, and the point is valid and well made. We are all players in the contract game, even if we do not realise it. In fact, we probably will not have any need to recognise that particular contractual version of reality until we enter into some transaction that goes wrong, or at least does not go as we hoped it would. Then, we seek to assert rights and to look for remedies against the person with whom we have come into dispute. It is at this time that the analytical framework of contract law principles comes to bear on the situation, to determine what, if any, rights can be enforced and what, if any, remedies can be recovered. It is perhaps paradoxical that students of contract law have to approach their study of the subject from the opposite end from that at which the layperson begins. The layperson wants a remedy and focuses on that above all else; the student, or practitioner, realises that the availability of the remedy depends upon establishing contractual responsibility and, hence, their focus is on the establishment of the contractual relationship and the breach of that relationship, before any question of remedies can be considered. Such is the nature and relationship of law and ordinary, everyday reality.

Although people have always exchanged goods, market transactions only came to be the dominant form of economic activity during the nineteenth century, even in the UK. The general law of contract as it now operates is essentially the product of the common law and emerged in the course of the nineteenth century. It has been suggested that the general principles of contract law, or the 'classical model of contract', as they are known, are themselves based on an idealised model of how the market operates.

DEFINITION (FOR WHAT IT IS WORTH)

Given the examples of contracts cited above, it may be appreciated that the simplest possible description of a contract is a 'legally binding agreement'. It should be noted, however, that, although all contracts are the outcome of agreements, not all agreements are contracts; that is, not all agreements are legally enforceable. In order to be in a position to determine whether a particular agreement will be enforced by the courts, one must have an understanding of the rules and principles of contract law.

The emphasis placed on agreement highlights the consensual nature of contracts. It is sometimes said that contract is based on *consensus ad idem*, that is, a meeting of minds. This is slightly misleading, however, for the reason that English contract law applies an objective test in determining whether or not a contract exists. It is not so much a matter of what the parties actually had in mind, as what their behaviour would lead others to conclude as to their state of mind. Consequently, contracts may be found and enforced, even though the parties themselves might not have thought that they had entered into such a relationship.

There is no *general* requirement that contracts be made in writing. They can be created by word of mouth or by action, as well as in writing. Contracts made in any of these ways are known as *simple* contracts. Some contracts, mainly relating to land, have to be made by deed and referred to as *speciality* contracts.

FORMATION OF A CONTRACT

As has been said, not every agreement, let alone every promise, will be enforced by the law. But what distinguishes the enforceable promise from the unenforceable one? The essential elements of a binding agreement/contract are:

- offer;
- acceptance;
- consideration;
- capacity; and
- intention to create legal relations.

OFFER

An offer is a promise to be bound on particular terms. The person who makes the offer is the offeror; the person who receives the offer is the offeree. The offer sets out the terms upon which the offeror is willing to enter into contractual relations with the offeree. An offer may, through acceptance by the offeree, result in a legally enforceable contract. It is important to be able to distinguish what the law will treat as an offer from other statements, which will not form the basis of an enforceable contract.

An offer must be distinguished from an *invitation to treat*, which occurs where someone asks another person to make an offer for something. The person making the invitation to treat is not bound to accept any offers made to them. The following are examples of common situations involving invitations to treat:

- the display of goods in a shop window;
- the display of goods on the shelf of a self-service shop;
- advertisements.

In none of these instances can the customer insist on the goods concerned being sold to them, let alone at the marked price.

Advertisements of goods on websites (internet shopping) are of particular interest. Some time ago the Argos website advertised Sony televisions at £2.99 instead of £299 and customers placed orders at £2.99. Customers mistakenly argued that they had accepted Argos' offer and that there was a binding contract to supply the goods for £2.99. However, there are exceptional circumstances where an advertisement may be treated as an offer; where the advertisement specifies performance of a task in return for a 'reward' and, on its terms, does not admit any room for negotiation.

An offer may be made to a particular person, or to a group of people, or to the whole world. If the offer is restricted, then only the people to whom it is addressed may accept it; if the offer is made to the public at large, it can be accepted by anyone. However, a person cannot accept an offer that he does not know about. Thus, if a person offers a reward for the return of a lost watch and someone returns it without knowing about the offer, he cannot claim the reward.

REJECTION AND REVOCATION OF OFFERS

If someone expressly rejects an offer, they cannot subsequently retract and accept the original offer. A counter-offer, where the offeree tries to change the terms of the offer, has the same effect.

Revocation, the technical term for cancellation, occurs when the offeror withdraws the offer. An offer may be revoked at any time before acceptance and once revoked, it is no longer open to the offeree to accept the original offer. However, the offeror must make sure that the offeree is made aware of the cancellation of the offer; otherwise it might still be open to the offeree to accept the offer. A promise to keep an offer open is only binding where there is a separate contract to that effect, known as an option contract.

A unilateral contract is one where one party promises something in return for some action on the part of another party. Rewards for finding lost property are examples of such unilateral promises. It would be unfair if the promisor were allowed to revoke their offer just before the offeree was about to complete their part of the contract, so in relation to unilateral contracts, revocation is not permissible once the offeree has started performing the task requested.

Offers lapse and are no longer capable of acceptance at the end of a stated period, or after a 'reasonable' time, where no time limit is set. What amounts to a reasonable time is, of course, dependent upon the particular circumstances of each case.

ACCEPTANCE

Acceptance of the offer is necessary for the formation of a contract. Once the offeree has agreed to the terms offered, a contract comes into effect. Both parties are bound: the offeror can no longer withdraw their offer and the offeree cannot withdraw their acceptance.

FORM OF ACCEPTANCE

In order to form a binding agreement, the acceptance must correspond with the terms of the offer. Thus, the offeree must not seek to introduce new contractual terms into the acceptance.

As has been seen already, a counter-offer does not constitute acceptance. Equally, a conditional acceptance cannot create a contract relationship. Thus, any agreement subject to contract is not binding, but merely signifies the fact that the parties are in the process of finalising the terms on which they will be willing to be bound. However, the mere fact that a person adds a 'qualification' to their acceptance may not prevent acceptance from taking place, as the exact legal effect is a question of fact in each case.

As with an offer, acceptance may be in the form of express words, either oral or written, or it may be implied from conduct.

COMMUNICATION OF ACCEPTANCE

The general rule is that acceptance must be communicated to the offeror and silence cannot amount to acceptance. So a letter to the effect that 'If I do not hear from you by next week I shall consider the agreement binding' has no legal merit.

There are, however, exceptions to the general rule that acceptance must be communicated, which arise in the following cases:

Where the offeror has waived the right to receive communication For
   example, in reward cases, those seeking to benefit do not have
   to inform the person offering the reward that they have begun

to perform; the acceptance occurs when they do what is required.

Where acceptance is through the postal service In such circumstances, acceptance is complete as soon as the letter, properly addressed and stamped, is posted. The contract is concluded, even if the letter subsequently fails to reach the offeror. This postal rule also applies to telegrams, but it does not apply when means of instantaneous communication are used. It follows that when acceptance is made by means of telephone, fax or telex, the offeror must actually receive the acceptance. Email is generally recognised as instantaneous communication, so the postal rule does not apply.

CONSIDERATION

English law does not enforce gratuitous promises unless they are made by deed. Consideration can be understood as the price paid for a promise. The element of bargain implicit in the idea of consideration is evident in the following definition by Sir Frederick Pollock, adopted by the House of Lords in *Dunlop v Selfridge* (1915): 'An act or forbearance of one party, or the promise thereof, is the price for which the promise of the other is bought, and the promise thus given for value is enforceable.'

It is sometimes said that consideration consists of some benefit to the promisor or detriment to the promisee. It should be noted that both elements stated in that definition are not required to be present to support a legally enforceable agreement though, in practice, they are usually present. If the promisee acts to their detriment, it is immaterial that the action does not directly benefit the promisor. However, that detriment must be suffered at the request of the promisor.

Consideration can be divided into the following categories:

- *Executory consideration*: This is the promise to perform an action at some future time. A contract can be made on the basis of an exchange of promises as to future action. Such a contract is known as an executory contract.
- *Executed consideration*: In the case of unilateral contracts, where the offeror promises something in return for the offeree's doing

something, the promise only becomes enforceable when the offeree has actually performed the required act.

- *Past consideration*: This category does not actually count as valid consideration. Consideration must be given because of or in return for the other's promise and as past consideration is action already wholly performed before the promise was made, it is not legally valid in contract law. There are exceptions, so where the claimant performed the action at the request of the defendant and payment was expected, then any subsequent promise to pay will be enforceable.

The rule that consideration must not be past, is only one of the many rules that govern the legal definition and operation of consideration. Other rules are as follows:

- *Performance must be legal* The courts will not countenance a claim to enforce a promise to pay for any criminal act.
- *Consideration must move from the promisee* If A promises B £1,000 if B gives his car to C, then C cannot usually enforce B's promise, because C is not the party who has provided the consideration for the promise. This is sometimes referred to as the doctrine of *privity*. Consequently, it is a general rule that a contract can only impose rights or obligations on persons who are parties to it. There are, however, common law individual exceptions and general rights are protected by the *Contracts (Rights of Third Parties) Act 1999*.
- *Consideration must be sufficient but need not be adequate* It is up to the parties themselves to decide the terms of their contract. The court will not intervene to require equality in the value exchanged; as long as the agreement has been freely entered into, and some valid consideration provided (i.e. *sufficient*), the consideration exchanged need not be of equal value to what is exchanged (i.e. *adequate*).

It has generally been accepted that performance of an existing duty, either of a public or an existing contractual nature, does not provide valid consideration for a further claim such as additional payment. However, if the party claiming has done more than they were bound to do, or the other party gains practical benefit from their action, then they can claim for any additional amount promised.

CAPACITY

Capacity refers to a person's ability to enter into a contract. In general, all adults of sound mind have full capacity. However, the capacity of certain individuals is limited.

MINORS

A minor is a person under the age of 18. The law tries to protect such persons by restricting their contractual capacity and, thus, preventing them from entering into disadvantageous agreements. The rules which apply are a mixture of common law and statute and depend on when the contract was made. Agreements entered into by minors may be classified within three possible categories:

MENTAL INCAPACITY AND INTOXICATION

A contract made by a party who is of unsound mind or under the influence of drink or drugs is *prima facie* valid. In order to avoid a contract, such a person must show:

- that their mind was so affected at the time that they were incapable of understanding the nature of their actions; and
- that the other party either knew or ought to have known of their disability.

The person claiming such incapacity, nonetheless, must pay a reasonable price for necessaries sold and delivered to them. The Sale of Goods Act 1979 specifically applies the same rules to such people as those that are applicable to minors.

INTENTION TO CREATE LEGAL RELATIONS

All of the aspects considered previously may well be present in a particular agreement, and yet there still may not be a contract. In order to limit the number of cases that might otherwise be brought, the courts will only enforce those agreements which the parties intended to have legal effect. Although expressed in terms of the parties' intentions, the test for the presence of such intention is once again objective, rather than subjective. For the purposes of this topic, agreements can be divided into three categories, in which different presumptions apply. It should be noted that, as with all presumptions, they may be rebutted by the actual circumstances of a particular case.

FAMILY AND SOCIAL AGREEMENTS

In this type of agreement, there is a presumption that the parties *do not* intend to create legal relations.

COMMERCIAL AGREEMENTS

In commercial situations, the strong presumption is that the parties intend to enter into a legally binding relationship in consequence of their dealings.

COLLECTIVE AGREEMENTS

Agreements between employers and trade unions may be considered as a distinct category of agreement for, although they are commercial agreements, they are presumed not to give rise to legal relations and, therefore, are not normally enforceable in the courts.

CONTENTS OF A CONTRACT

The foregoing has examined how to make a contract; this part looks at what is, or is not, contained in such an agreement. As the parties will normally be bound to perform any promise that they have contracted to undertake, it is important to decide precisely what promises are included in the contract.

REPRESENTATIONS

Some statements do not form part of a contract, even though they might have induced the other party to enter into the contract. These pre-contractual statements are called *representations*. The consequences of such representations being false will be an action for *misrepresentation*. The misrepresentation renders the contract voidable, i.e. the innocent party may rescind the contract or, in some circumstances, claim damages (see below for an explanation of these).

Misrepresentation can be divided into two types:

FRAUDULENT MISREPRESENTATION

In the case of fraudulent misrepresentation, the statement is made knowing it to be false, or believing it to be false, or recklessly careless as to whether it is true or false. The difficulty with this type of misrepresentation is proving the necessary mental element; it is notoriously difficult to show the required *mens rea*, or guilty mind, to demonstrate fraud.

NEGLIGENT MISREPRESENTATION

In his case the statement is made in the belief that it is true, but *without reasonable grounds* for that belief. There are two categories of negligent misrepresentation:

- *At common law* Prior to 1963, the law did not recognise a concept of negligent misrepresentation. The possibility of liability in negligence for misstatements arose from *Hedley Byrne & Co v Heller and Partners* (1964).
- *Under the Misrepresentation Act (MA) 1967* Although it might still be necessary, or beneficial, to sue at common law, it is more likely that such claims would now be taken under the statute. The reason for this is that s. 2(1) of the MA 1967 reverses the normal burden of proof so it becomes up to the party who made the statement to show that they had reasonable grounds for believing it to be true.

TERMS

Where a statement is of such major importance that the promisee would not have entered into the agreement without it, it will be construed as a term. Once it is decided that a statement is a term it is necessary to determine which type of term it is, in order to determine what remedies are available for its breach. Terms can be classified as one of three types.

CONDITIONS

A condition is a fundamental part of the agreement and is something which goes to the root of the contract. Breach of a condition gives the innocent party the right, either to terminate the contract and refuse to perform their part of it, or to go through with the agreement and sue for damages.

WARRANTIES

A warranty is a subsidiary obligation which is not vital to the overall agreement and does not totally destroy its efficacy. *Breach of a warranty does not give the right to terminate the agreement.* The innocent party has to complete their part of the agreement and can only sue for damages.

INNOMINATE TERMS

In this case, the remedy is not prescribed in advance simply by whether the term breached is a condition or a warranty, but depends on the consequence of the breach. If the breach deprives the innocent party of substantially the whole benefit of the contract, then the right to repudiate will be permitted, even if the term might otherwise appear to be a mere warranty. If, however, the innocent party does not lose the whole benefit of the contract, then they will not be permitted to repudiate but must settle for damages, even if the term might otherwise appear to be a condition.

IMPLIED TERMS

Implied terms, as the title suggests, are not actually stated but are introduced into the contract by implication. Implied terms can be divided into three types.

TERMS IMPLIED BY STATUTE

For example, under the SoGA 1979, terms relating to description, quality and fitness for purpose are all implied into sale of goods contracts.

TERMS IMPLIED BY CUSTOM

An agreement may be subject to customary terms not actually specified by the parties. Custom, however, cannot override the express terms of an agreement.

TERMS IMPLIED BY THE COURTS

Generally the court will presume that the parties intended to include a term which is not expressly stated. It will do so where it is necessary to give business efficacy to the contract.

EXEMPTION OR EXCLUSION CLAUSES

In a sense, an exemption clause is no different from any other clause, in that it seeks to define the rights and obligations of the parties to a contract. However, an exemption clause is a term in a contract which tries to exempt, or limit, the liability of a party in breach of the agreement. Exclusion clauses give rise to most concern when they are included in *standard form contracts*, in which one party, who is in a position of commercial dominance, imposes their terms on the other party, who has no choice (other than to take it or leave it) as far as the terms of the contract go. Such standard form contracts are contrary to the ideas of consensus and negotiation underpinning contract law; for this reason, they have received particular attention from both the judiciary and the legislature, in an endeavour to counteract their perceived unfairness.

The actual law relating to exclusion clauses is complicated by the interplay of the common law, the Unfair Contract Terms Act (UCTA) 1977 and the various Acts which imply certain terms into particular contracts. However, the following questions should always be asked with regard to exclusion clauses:

HAS THE EXCLUSION CLAUSE BEEN INCORPORATED INTO THE CONTRACT?

An exclusion clause cannot be effective unless it is actually a term of a contract. There are three ways in which such a term may be inserted into a contractual agreement:

- *By signature*: If a person signs a contractual document then they are bound by its terms, even if they do not read it.
- *By notice*: In order for notice to be adequate, the document bearing the exclusion clause must be an integral part of the contract and must be given at the time that the contract is made.
- *By custom*: Where the parties have had previous dealings on the basis of an exclusion clause, that clause may be included in later contracts.

DOES THE EXCLUSION CLAUSE EFFECTIVELY COVER THE BREACH?

As a consequence of the disfavour with which the judiciary have looked on exclusion clauses, a number of rules of construction have been developed which operate to restrict the effectiveness of exclusion clauses.

WHAT EFFECT DO UCTA 1977 AND THE UNFAIR TERMS IN CONSUMER CONTRACTS REGULATIONS 1999 HAVE ON THE EXCLUSION CLAUSE?

This legislation represents the statutory attempt to control exclusion clauses. In spite of its title, it is really aimed at unfair exemption clauses, rather than contract terms generally. The controls under UCTA 1977 relate to two areas:

NEGLIGENCE There is an absolute prohibition on exemption clauses in relation to liability in negligence resulting in death or injury (ss 2 and 5). Exemption clauses relating to liability for other damage caused by negligence will only be enforced to the extent that they satisfy the requirement of reasonableness (s. 5).

CONTRACT The general rule of the Act (s. 3) is that an exclusion clause imposed on a consumer (as defined in s. 12(1)) or by standard terms of business is not binding unless it satisfies the Act's requirement of reasonableness. 'The requirement of reasonableness means fair and reasonable ... having regard to the circumstances ... [s. 11].' Schedule 2 to UCTA 1977 provides guidelines for the application of the reasonableness test in regard to non-consumer transactions, but it is likely that similar considerations will be taken into account by the courts in consumer transactions. Amongst these considerations are:

(i)   the relative strength of the parties' bargaining power;
(ii) whether any inducement was offered in return for the limitation on liability.

DISCHARGE OF A CONTRACT

When a contract is discharged, the parties to the agreement are freed from their contractual obligations. A contract is discharged in one of four ways:

- agreement;
- performance;
- frustration; or
- breach.

Of these agreement is the most usual, but breach is probably the most important for lawyers.

DISCHARGE BY AGREEMENT

Emphasis has been placed on the consensual nature of contract law, and it follows that what has been made by agreement can be ended by agreement. The contract itself may contain provision for its discharge by either the passage of a fixed period of time or the occurrence of a particular event.

DISCHARGE BY PERFORMANCE

This occurs where the parties to a contract perform their obligations under it. Performance is the normal way in which contracts are discharged. As a general rule, discharge requires complete and exact performance of the obligations in the contract. Where the essential element of an agreement has been performed but some minor part or fault remains to be done or remedied, the party who performed the act can claim the contract price, although they remain liable for any deduction for the work outstanding. Partial performance occurs in the following circumstances: A orders a case of 12 bottles of oil from B. B only has 10, and delivers those to A. A is at liberty to reject the 10 bottles if they want to; once the goods are accepted, though, they must pay a proportionate price for them. If a buyer refuses to accept the goods offered (where there are no legal grounds to do so, for example, where the goods are not defective), but later sues for breach of contract, the seller can rely on the fact that they 'tendered performance' as discharging their liability under the contract.

DISCHARGE BY FRUSTRATION

The doctrine of frustration allows a party to a contract to be excused performance on the grounds of impossibility arising after formation of the contract.

For example, a contract will be discharged by reason of frustration where destruction of the subject matter of the contract has occurred or where the commercial purpose of the contract is defeated. (This applies where the circumstances have so changed that to hold a party to their promise would require them to do something which, although not impossible, would be radically different from the original agreement.)

DISCHARGE BY BREACH

Breach of a contract occurs where one of the parties to the agreement fails to comply, either completely or satisfactorily, with their obligations under it. A breach of contract may occur in three ways:

- where a party, prior to the time of performance, states that they will not fulfil their contractual obligation. This *anticipatory* breach may be express, where a party states that they will not perform their contractual obligations, or *implied*, where a party does something else, which makes future performance impossible.
- where a party fails to perform their contractual obligation; or
- where a party performs their obligation in a defective manner.

EFFECT OF BREACH

Any breach will result in the innocent party being able to sue for damages. In addition, however, some breaches will permit the innocent party to treat the contract as having been discharged. In this situation, they can refuse either to perform their part of the contract or to accept further performance from the party in breach. The right to treat a contract as discharged arises in the following instances, where the other party:

- has repudiated the contract before performance is due, or before they have completed performance; or
- has committed a fundamental breach of contract (see above).

REMEDIES FOR BREACH OF CONTRACT

The principal remedies for breach of contract are:

- damages;
- *quantum meruit*;
- specific performance;
- injunction;
- action for the agreed contract price; and
- repudiation.

DAMAGES

Damages are the monetary compensation for breach of contract. The estimation of what damages are to be paid by a party in breach of contract can be divided into two parts: remoteness and measure.

REMOTENESS OF DAMAGE   What kind of damage can the innocent party claim for? This involves a consideration of causation and the remoteness of cause from effect, in order to determine how far down a chain of events a defendant is liable. The general rule is that damages will only be awarded in respect of losses *which arise naturally*, that is, in the natural course of things; or which both parties may reasonably be supposed to have contemplated as a probable result of its breach, when the contract was made.

The effect of the first part of the rule is that the party in breach is deemed to expect the normal consequences of the breach, whether they actually expected them or not.

Under the second part of the rule, however, the party in breach can only be held liable for abnormal consequences where they have actual knowledge that the abnormal consequences might follow.

As a consequence of the test for remoteness, a party may be liable for consequences which, although within the reasonable contemplation of the parties, are much more serious in effect than would be expected of them.

MEASURE OF DAMAGES   Damages in contract are intended to compensate an injured party for any financial loss sustained as a consequence of another party's breach. The object is not to punish the party in breach, so the amount of damages awarded can never be greater than the actual loss suffered. The aim is to put the injured party in the same position they would have been in had the contract been properly performed. There are a number of procedures which seek to achieve this end, as follows:

- *The market rule* This means that if goods are not delivered under a contract, the buyer is entitled to go into the market and buy similar goods, paying the market price prevailing at the time.

They can then claim the difference in price between what they paid and the original contract price as damages. Conversely, if a buyer refuses to accept goods under a contract, the seller can sell the goods in the market and accept the prevailing market price. Any difference between the price they receive and the contract price can be claimed in damages

- *The duty to mitigate losses* The injured party is under a duty to take all reasonable steps to minimise their loss. So, in the above examples, the buyer of goods which are not delivered has to buy the replacements as cheaply as possible, and the seller of goods which are not accepted has to try to get as good a price as they can when they sell them.

At one time, damages could not be recovered where the loss sustained through breach of contract was of a non-financial nature, but the contemporary position is that such non-pecuniary damages can be recovered.

LIQUIDATED DAMAGES AND PENALTIES   It is possible, and common in business contracts, for the parties to an agreement to make provisions for possible breach by stating in advance the amount of damages that will have to be paid in the event of any breach occurring. Damages under such a provision are known as liquidated damages. They will only be recognised by the court if they represent a genuine pre-estimate of loss and are not intended to operate as a penalty against the party in breach. If the court considers the provision to be a penalty, it will not give it effect but will award damages in the normal way.

QUANTUM MERUIT   The term *quantum meruit* means that a party should be awarded as much as he had earned, and such an award can be either contractual or quasi-contractual (see below) in nature. Payment may also be claimed on the basis of *quantum meruit* where a party has carried out work in respect of a void contract and the other party has accepted that work.

SPECIFIC PERFORMANCE   It will sometimes suit a party to break their contractual obligations and pay damages. Through an order for specific performance, however, the party in breach may be instructed to complete their part of the contract. The following rules govern the award of specific performance:

- it will only be granted in cases where the common law remedy of damages is inadequate. It is not usually applied to contracts concerning the sale of goods where replacements are readily available. It is most commonly granted in cases involving the sale of land and where the subject matter of the contract is unique (for example, a painting by Picasso);
- it will not be granted where the court cannot supervise its enforcement. For this reason, it will not be available in respect of contracts of employment or personal service;
- As it is an equitable remedy, specific performance will not be granted where the claimant has not acted properly; neither will it be granted where mutuality is lacking. Thus, a minor will not be granted specific performance, because no such order could be awarded against a minor.

INJUNCTION

This is also another equitable order of the court, which directs a person not to break their contract. An injunction will only be granted to enforce negative covenants within the agreement and cannot be used to enforce positive obligations.

ACTION FOR THE AGREED CONTRACT PRICE

In some circumstances, a party may sue for non-payment of the price rather than seeking damages for breach.

QUASI-CONTRACTUAL REMEDIES

Quasi-contractual remedies are based on the assumption that a person should not receive any undue advantage from the fact that there is no contractual remedy to force them to account for it. An important quasi-contractual remedy is an action for money paid and received.

If no contract comes into existence by reason of a total failure of consideration, then, under this action, any goods or money received will have to be returned to the party who supplied them.

Our look at the law of contract has covered many areas of rules. In sum, these rules can be seen as being at the heart of that part of the legal system that governs the way citizens and organisations make enforceable agreements. That is something central to the way our whole society works.

GLOSSARY

We are pleased to acknowledge the Glossary of the Judiciary of England and Wales for many of the entries here.

A posteriori   In the context of reasoning, proving the cause from the effect, e.g. seeing a watch and concluding there was a watchmaker, or, like Robinson Crusoe, seeing a footprint on a desert island and inferring the presence of another person. This is inductive reasoning.

A priori   Reasoning from a general principle to a necessary effect, and where you do not need to wait until after an event to assert a truth, e.g. dead people do not breathe.

Act   A law made in Parliament, also called a statute. An Act sets out legal rules, and has normally been passed by both Houses of Parliament in the form of a Bill and agreed to by the Crown.

Adjournment   A temporary postponement of legal proceedings.

ADR   Alternative Dispute Resolution. Methods of resolving disputes which do not involve the normal trial process.

Advocate   A lawyer, who speaks for a client in a court of law.

Aggravating   Factors making a situation worse. For example, burglary is aggravated in the eyes of a court if the burglar is armed, or injures someone while committing the offence.

Alibi (Latin for elsewhere) A defence that someone accused of a crime was not there at the time and could not have committed the offence.

Appeal A formal request to a higher court that the verdict or ruling or sentence of a court be changed.

ASBO Anti-social Behaviour Orders. These are court orders which prohibit specific anti-social behaviours. An ASBO is issued for a minimum of two years, and can ban an offender from visiting certain areas, mixing with certain people or carrying on the offending behaviour. Despite being issued by a court, an ASBO is a civil order, not a criminal penalty – this means it won't appear on an individual's criminal record. However, breaching an ASBO is a criminal offence punishable by a fine or up to five years in prison. In 2011, the government announced plans to abolish the ASBO.

Bail Release of a defendant from custody until their next appearance in court. This can be subject to security being given and/or compliance with certain conditions, such as a curfew.

BAILII The British and Irish Legal Information Institute, which provides free access to the British and Irish primary legal materials on the internet, including a wide variety of court judgments.

The Bar Barristers are 'called to the Bar' when they have finished their training, and as a result are then allowed to represent clients. The Bar is also a collective term for all barristers, represented by the General Council of the Bar.

Barrister A barrister is a legal practitioner in England, Wales and Northern Ireland. The name comes from the process of being called to the Bar after being trained. Barristers represent individuals in court, and provide them with specialist legal advice. Barristers must usually be instructed (hired) through a solicitor, but a change to the rules in 2004 means that members of the public may now approach a barrister directly in certain circumstances.

The Bench Judges or magistrates sitting in court are collectively known as 'the Bench'.

Bill A draft of a proposed law presented to Parliament. Once agreed by Parliament and given Royal Assent by the ruling monarch, Bills become law and are known as Acts.

Binding/bound over   Being placed under a legal obligation, for example being 'bound over' to keep the peace. Failure to observe a binding order may result in a penalty.

CAFCASS   The Children and Family Court Advisory and Support Service. CAFCASS looks after the interests of children involved in proceedings in the family courts in England and Wales and works with children and their families to advise the courts on children's best interests in family cases, be that in divorce and separation, adoption, or child care and supervision proceedings.

Case law   The body of law created by judges' decisions on individual cases.

Cessante ratione legis, cessat lex ipsa   When the reason for its existence ceases, the law itself ceases to exist. Truer of common law than of legislation.

Circuit judge   A judge who normally sits in the county court and/or Crown Court.

Civil court   A court that deals with matters concerning private rights and not offences against the state.

Chambers   This has two meanings: a private room or courtroom from which the public are excluded, in which a judge may conduct certain sorts of hearings, for example family cases; or offices used by a barrister.

Compensation   A sum of money paid to make amends for loss, damage, hardship, inconvenience or personal injury caused by another.

Constitutional Reform Act   The Constitutional Reform Act, which was granted Royal Assent on 24 March 2005, reformed the office of Lord Chancellor, established the Lord Chief Justice as head of the judiciary of England and Wales and President of the Courts of England and Wales, and created the Supreme Court of the United Kingdom. In addition the Act also made provision for the creation of a Judicial Appointments Commission, an Office of Judicial Complaints, and a Judicial Appointments and Conduct Ombudsman.

Contempt of court   An offence that can lead to a fine and even imprisonment because of a lack of respect or obedience by an individual in a court of law. You are also in contempt of court if you disobey an injunction or court order.

Counsel   A barrister.

The Crown   The institution of the monarchy, or the historical power of the monarchy, usually exercised today through government and courts. It is the Crown which brings all criminal cases to court, via the Crown Prosecution Service.

Crown Court   The Crown Court deals with all crime committed for trial by magistrates' courts. Cases for trial are heard before a judge and jury. The Crown Court also acts as an appeal court for cases heard and dealt with by magistrates.

Cui bono?   'to whom good?' In other words, who stands to gain? Used by the ancient Roman lawyer Cicero. In trying to solve a mystery or crime it is often useful to look for someone who would stand to gain by the event.

Culpability   Blame.

Curfew   A legal order confining someone to their home, sometimes for set times of the day.

Custodial sentence   Where an offender is confined to a prison or young offenders' institution for a set period of time.

Damnum sine injuria esse potest   There can be damage (such as physical injury or financial loss) without there being a legal wrong.

DCA   (Department for Constitutional Affairs), the Department formerly responsible for running the courts and improving the justice system, human rights and information rights law, and law and policy on running elections and modernising the constitution. The Ministry of Justice was established on 9 May 2007 and is now responsible for policy on the overall criminal, civil, family and administrative justice system, including sentencing policy, as well as the courts, tribunals, legal aid and constitutional reform.

Defendant   A person who appears in court because they are being sued, standing trial or appearing for sentence.

De minimis non curat lex   The law does not concern itself with the smallest, trivial matters.

Disclosure   A three-tiered system in criminal proceedings which ensures vital information on both sides of a court case can be seen by all parties:

- Primary disclosure is the duty of the prosecutor to disclose material to the defence that undermines the case against the accused. Primary disclosure is triggered where the accused faces trial in a magistrates' court and pleads not guilty, or the case is transferred for trial by jury;

- A defence statement sets out the general nature of the defence, indicating matters on which the accused takes issues with the prosecution and why. A defence statement is compulsory for an accused facing trial by jury, and is optional for an accused facing a summary trial;

- Secondary disclosure takes place as soon as possible after receiving a defence statement, and provides details of any information which had not previously been disclosed and which might reasonably be expected to assist the accused's defence as set out in the defence statement.

In civil proceedings, all relevant documents have to be disclosed unless they are governed by privilege (see below).

District Judge (Magistrate)   Known as stipendiary magistrates before 2000, district judges are full-time members of the judiciary and deal with a broad range of cases appearing before magistrates' courts – especially the lengthier and more complex criminal cases and care cases relating to children. They may sit with lay magistrates or alone.

District judges   Formerly known as County Court Registrars, district judges sit in the county courts or district registries in a specific region. Much of the work of district judges is in chambers, and they have the power to try actions in a county court below a specified financial limit which is reviewed from time to time. Cases above that limit are generally heard by a circuit judge. District judges also act as arbitrators in the county courts, hear matrimonial cases and deal with nearly all the preliminary stages in civil and family proceedings and pre-trial reviews. Some also determine cases involving children.

Draft Bill   An early version of a proposed Bill before it is introduced into Parliament.

Embezzlement   Dishonestly appropriating another's assets for one's own use.

Feme covert   (pronounced femm cuvert) a married woman (from the Latin *femina viro co-operta*).

Feme sole   (pronounced femm soul) a single woman, including those who have been married.

Fraud   An act or instance of deception.

Gavel   A small mallet used to signal for attention. One of the most famous symbols of the judiciary, but ironically, they are not and never have been used in English or Welsh courtrooms.

Hearing   Proceedings held before a court.

High Court   A civil court consisting of three divisions: the Queen's Bench, which deals with civil disputes including breach of contract, personal injuries, commercial and building cases, libel or slander; Family, which is concerned with matrimonial matters and proceedings relating to children or adults who cannot make decisions for themselves; and Chancery, which deals with property matters including fraud and bankruptcy.

Home Office   The government department responsible for internal affairs, including crime, in England and Wales.

Independence of the judiciary   Public confidence in the judiciary requires that judges decide cases according to law and not according to bribery, threats or political pressure. Various rules promote free and fearless judging – judicial salaries are not annually approved by Parliament, and judges can't be sued for any judicial utterances.

JCO   The Judicial Communications Office, which exists to enhance public confidence in the judiciary for England and Wales, advises members of the judiciary on media matters and helps them communicate with each other.

JP   Justice of the Peace. The official title of a magistrate.

Judiciary   Collective term for the 43,000 judges, magistrates and tribunal members who deal with legal matters in England and Wales.

Law Commission   Independent body set up by Parliament to review and recommend reform of the law in England and Wales.

Law Lord   The unofficial title of the former Lords of Appeal in Ordinary (now Justices of the Supreme Court) who delivered opinions in the House of Lords, the highest court for England and Wales before October 2009.

Lawyer   General term for someone practising law, such as a solicitor or barrister.

Lord Chief Justice   Head of the judiciary of England and Wales and President of the Courts of England and Wales.

Magistrate   Magistrates are members of the public who voluntarily give up their time to act as lay judges in magistrates' courts. They need have no formal legal qualifications, although they are trained in court procedures.

Magistrates' courts   The magistrates' courts are a key part of the criminal justice system – virtually all criminal cases start in a magistrates' court and over 95 per cent of cases are also completed here. In addition, magistrates' courts deal with many civil cases, mostly family matters. Cases in the magistrates' courts are usually heard by panels of three magistrates (Justices of the Peace), of which there are around 28,000 in England and Wales.

Mediation   Process taking place outside a court to resolve a dispute.

Misfeasance   An old term meaning the unlawful performance of a lawful act. As opposed to malfeasance (certain sorts of intrinsically unlawful conduct), or nonfeasance (an omission to do something that should by law be done).

Mitigation   Arguments made on behalf of a defendant who has admitted or been found guilty of an offence, in order to excuse or partly excuse the offence committed and attempt to minimise the sentence.

MoJ   The Ministry of Justice was established on 9 May 2007. It has responsibility for the courts, sentencing, prisons, rehabilitation plus former DCA policies like voting, crown dependencies, human rights, tribunals and freedom of information.

Open court   The vast majority of hearings in England and Wales are held in open court, with members of the public free to enter the courtroom and observe proceedings. Some sensitive cases, such as family matters, may be held 'in camera', which means 'in the chamber' or in private.

Parliamentary sovereignty   The highest power in British democracy is that of the electorate – expressed through its representatives in Parliament. This is the supreme (or 'sovereign') power. Legislation can be used to make any imaginable law. In 1917, Lord Justice Scrutton contemplated that a statute could make 'two plus two equal to five'. Some economists, though, have been doing that for a while.

Plea and case management hearings   A preliminary hearing, before a judge at a crown court, where the accused may indicate whether or not they plan to plead guilty and have the chance to argue that there is insufficient evidence for the case to go before a jury. Directions are also given on matters such as what evidence will be admitted.

Preferment   Advancing to a higher rank; another term for promotion.

Pre-trial hearing   A short court hearing at which a judge considers how ready all parties in a case may be for the trial and fixes a timetable where necessary.

Privilege   The right of a party to refuse to disclose a document or produce a document or to refuse to answer questions on the ground of some special interest recognised by law.

Probate   The legal recognition of the validity of a will.

Prosecution   The conduct of criminal proceedings against a person.

Pupillage   The final stage of training to be a barrister. It usually takes a year to complete, with the year divided into two six-month periods spent working in a set of chambers.

QC   Barristers and solicitors with sufficient experience and knowledge can apply to become Queen's Counsel. QCs undertake work of an important nature and are referred to as 'silks', a name derived from the black court gown that is worn. QCs will be known as King's Counsel if a king assumes the throne.

Quis custodiet ipsos custodes?   Who shall guard the guards? i.e. even guards and protectors can be deficient.

Recorder   A Recordership appointment, which carries almost the same powers as a circuit judge, is made by the Queen, and lasts for five years. Recorders generally sit for between four and six weeks a year, and normally spend the rest of the time in private practice as barristers or solicitors.

Rule of law   This is a defining characteristic of civilised democracies. Famously articulated by the Victorian jurist A.V. Dicey, the principle means that everyone, however powerful, must obey the democratically passed law, and no one is above the law. The rules are more important than important people. We are ruled by the rules not by rulers.

Separation of powers   Rooted in ideas of Aristotle, and popularised by the French writer Montesquieu, this precept notes that there are three types of governmental function: legislative, executive and judicial. If more than one of those is given to one person or agency, it is a threat to the freedom of citizens. Not rigidly applicable in the UK as, for example, the Supreme Court Justices are judicial but can 'legislate' in the sense that they can make new law by declaring that it is time for the common law to develop, and then changing the law.

Statutory law   A law that has been passed by an Act of Parliament.

Summary trial   Trial taking place in a magistrates' court.

Suppressio veri, suggestio falsi   The deliberate suppression of truth implies something untrue. The cold cost of being 'economical with the truth'.

Supreme Court   The Supreme Court was created under the terms of the Constitutional Reform Act 2005, established in 2009, and completes the separation of the UK's legal and judicial systems. Justices of the Supreme Court do not sit or vote in the House of Lords. Slightly confusingly, the High Court and Court of Appeal were, prior to 2009, referred to as the Supreme Court – today they are called the 'Senior Courts of England and Wales'.

Suspended sentence   A custodial sentence, but one which will not result in time spent in custody unless another offence is committed within a specified period.

Time immemorial   Time beyond legal memory. For legal purposes this is taken to be from the accession of Richard I, in 1189. In English law a custom can today be obligatory on those within its scope if its practice can be shown to have existed since time immemorial. The choice of 1189 as the starting point for legal memory was made by the Statute of Westminster in 1275 which fixed that date as the earliest in respect of which actions about certain land ownership disputes could be brought.

Tort   A civil wrong committed against a person for which compensation may be sought through a civil court, e.g. cases of personal injury, negligent driving and libel.

Tribunal   Tribunals are an important part of the judicial system, but function outside of courtrooms. There are nearly 100 different tribunals in England and Wales, each dedicated to a specific area – from pensions appeals to asylum and VAT matters. It is an extremely diverse system – the largest tribunal hears over 300,000 cases a year, while some rarely sit. Some are based on a presidential structure, while some are regional; some panels are legally qualified, some are not. Some tribunals are very formal, with legal representation common, but many are not.

Uphold/upheld   Where an appeal against a judicial decision ends with the original ruling being maintained.

Ward of court   A minor (under 18) who is the subject of a wardship order. The order ensures that the court has custody, with day-to-day care carried out by an individual(s) or local authority. As long as the minor remains a ward of court, all decisions regarding the minor's upbringing must be approved by the court, e.g. transfer to a different school, or medical treatment.

Wardship   A High Court action making a minor a ward of court.

YJB   The Youth Justice Board for England and Wales oversees the youth justice system and works to prevent offending and reoffending by children and young people under the age of 18, to ensure that custody for them is safe and secure, and to address the causes of their offending behaviour.

BIBLIOGRAPHY

Abel-Smith, Brian and Robert Stevens (1967) *Lawyers and the Courts*, London: Heinemann.

Adler, Stephen (1995) *The Jury: Disorder in the Court*, New York: Main Street Books.

Allen, Sir Carleton Kemp (1927) *Law in the Making*, Oxford: The Clarendon Press.

Aquinas, Thomas (1225–74) *Summa Theologiae*.

Archbold (2006) *Criminal Pleading Evidence and Practice*, London: Sweet & Maxwell.

Baker, John Hamilton (2005) *The Oxford History of the Laws of England*, Vol. I, Oxford: Oxford University Press.

Bentham, Jeremy (1970 [1780]) *An Introduction to the Principles and Morals of Legislation*, ed. J. H. Burns and H. L. A. Hart, New York: Oceana.

——(1975 [1864]) *The Theory of Legislation*, ed. Upendra Baxi, New York: Oceana.

Blackstone, William (2001 [1765–69]) *Commentaries on the Laws of England*, ed. Wayne Morrison, London: Cavendish Publishing.

Bogdanor, Vernon (2004) 'Our New Constitution', *120 Law Quarterly Review*, 242–62.

Bogdanor, Vernon (ed.) (2005) *The British Constitution in the Twentieth Century*, Oxford: Oxford University Press.

Bradley, A. W. and K. D. Ewing (2002) *Constitutional and Administrative Law*, Harlow: Pearson.

Bromley, P. M. (1976) *Family Law*, London: Butterworths.

Carroll, Lewis (1996 [1872]) *Through the Looking Glass – And What Alice Found There*, London: Macmillan.

Cicero (2000) *Defence Speeches*, translation by D. H. Berry, Oxford: Oxford University Press.

Darbyshire, Penny (1991) 'The Lamp That Shows That Freedom Lives – Is It Worth the Candle?' *Criminal Law Review* 740 (October).

De Mello, Rambert (ed.) (2000) *Human Rights Act 1998*, Bristol: Jordan Publishing.

Denning, Lord (1979) *The Discipline of Law*, London: Butterworths.

——(1980) *The Due Process of Law*, London: Butterworths.

——(1983) *The Closing Chapter*, London: Butterworths.

——(1984) *Landmarks in the Law*, London: Butterworths.

Devlin, Sir Patrick (1965) *The Enforcement of Morals*, Oxford: Oxford University Press.

——(1966) *Trial By Jury* (The Hamlyn Lectures), London: Stevens.

Dicey, A. V. (1893 [1885]) *Introduction to the Study of the Law of the Constitution*, London: Macmillan.

——(2001 [1905]) *Lectures on the Relation Between Law and Public Opinion in England During the Nineteenth Century*, University Press of the Pacific.

Durkheim, Emile (1984 [1893]) *The Division of Labour in Society*, Basingstoke: Macmillan.

Edwards, J. (1964) *The Law Officers of the Crown*, London: Sweet & Maxwell.

Engels, Frederick (1969 [1845]) *The Condition of the Working Class in England*, London: Panther.

France, Anatole (1923 [1894]) *Le Lys Rouge*, Paris: Calmann-Levy.

Frankfurter, Felix (1965) *Of Men and Law: Papers and Addresses of Felix Frankfurter 1939–1956*, ed. Philip Elman, North Haven, CT: Archon Books.

Furmston, Michael (1981) 'Ignorance of the Law', *Legal Studies*, Vol. 1, 36–55.

Gray, John (2002) *Lawyers' Latin: a Vade-Mecum*, London: Robert Hale.

Gray, Kevin and Susan Francis Gray (2001) *Land Law*, London: Butterworths.

Green, Kate and Joe Cursley (2001) *Land Law*, Basingstoke: Palgrave.

Griffith, J. A. G. (1977) *The Politics of the Judiciary*, London: Fontana.

Grove, Trevor (1998) *The Juryman's Tale*, London: Bloomsbury.

——(2002) *The Magistrate's Tale*, London: Bloomsbury.

Hamson, Charles (1955) *The Law: Its Study and Comparison*, Cambridge: Cambridge University Press.

Hansen, M. N. (1999) *The Athenian Democracy in the Age of Demosthenes*, Bristol: Classical Press.

Harding, A. (1996) *A Social History of England*, Harmondsworth: Penguin.

Harris, Brian (2006) *Injustice: State Trials from Socrates to Nuremberg*, Stroud: Sutton Publishing.

Hart, H. L. A. (1961) *The Concept of Law*, Oxford: Clarendon Press.

Herbert, A. P. (1969 [1935]) *Uncommon Law*, London: Methuen.

Judicial Studies Board (2005–08) *Strategy*, London: Department for Constitutional Affairs.

Lee, Harper (1997 [1960]) *To Kill a Mocking Bird*, London: Arrow Books.

Lidstone, K. W., R. Hogg and F. Sutcliffe (1980) *Prosecutions by Private Individuals and Non-Police Agencies*, London: HMSO.

Lloyd, Denis (1964) *The Idea of Law*, Harmondsworth: Penguin.

Maine, Henry (1905 [186]) *Ancient Law*, London: John Murray.

Malleson, K. (1999) *The New Judiciary – the effect of expansion and activism*, Aldershot: Ashgate.

Markesinis, B. S. and S. F. Deakin (1999) *Tort Law*, Oxford: Clarendon Press.

Matthews, Paul and John Foreman (eds) (1993) *Jervis on Coroners*, London: Sweet & Maxwell.

McKendrick, Ewan (2003) *Contract Law*, Basingstoke: Macmillan.

Megarry, R. E. (1973) *A Second Miscellany-at-Law*, London: Stevens & Sons Ltd.

——(2005) *A New Miscellany-at-Law*, Oxford: Hart Publishing,

More, Sir Thomas (2004 [1516]) *Utopia* (translation by Paul Turner), London: Penguin.

Norrie, A. (1993) *Crime, Reason and History*, London: Butterworths.

Oliver, Dawn and Gavin Drewry (eds) (1998) *The Law and Parliament*, London: Butterworths.

Pollock, F. and F. W. Maitland (1968) *History of English Law*, (second edn), Volume 1, Cambridge: Cambridge University Press.

Radzinowicz, Leon (1956) *A History of English Criminal Law*, Vols. I, II, London: Stevens & Sons.

Reid, Lord (1972) 'The Judge as Law Maker', *Journal of the Society of Public Teachers of Law* 22.

Rose, David (1996) *In the Name of the Law*, London: Jonathan Cape.

Sanders, A. (1997) 'Criminal Justice: the development of criminal justice research in Britain', in P. Thomas (ed.), *Socio-Legal Studies*, Aldershot: Dartmouth, 185–205.

Sharpe, J. A. (1984) *Crime in Early Modern Britain 1550–1750*, London: Longman.

Shetreet, Shimon (1976) *Judges on Trial: A Study of the Appointment and Accountability of the English Judiciary*, Amsterdam: North-Holland Publishing Company.

Sigler, J. A. (1974) 'Public Prosecutions in England and Wales', *Criminal Law Review*, 642–51.

Simpson, A. W. B. (1988) *Invitation to Law*, Oxford: Blackwell.

——(1995) *Leading Cases in the Common Law*, Oxford: Clarendon Press.

Stafford, R. J. (1989) *Private Prosecutions*, London: Shaw & Sons.

Stein, P. (1984) *Legal Institutions*, London: Butterworths.

——(1999) *Roman Law in European History*, Cambridge: Cambridge University Press.

Strickland, Rennard (1997) 'The Cinematic Lawyer: the Magic Mirror and the Silver Screen', *Oklahoma City University Law Review*, 22 (1): 13.

Symonds, Arthur (ed.) (1989 [1835]) *The Mechanics of Law Making*, Cambridge: Chadwyck-Healey in association with the British Library and Avero Publications.

Thompson, E. P. (1975) *Whigs and Hunters: the origin of the Black Act*, Harmondsworth: Penguin.

Wendell Holmes, Oliver (1991 [1881]) *The Common Law*, New York: Dover Publications.

Williams, Glanville (1983) *Textbook of Criminal Law*, London: Stevens.

INDEX